Word-Power

33 Ways to write more convincing emails, blogs and books.

Includes Right/Left Brain Perception Tips

John Krone

Word-Power

33 Ways to write more convincing emails, blogs and books.

By John Krone

Contents

Preface *(About me.)*

Hi! I'm John Krone.

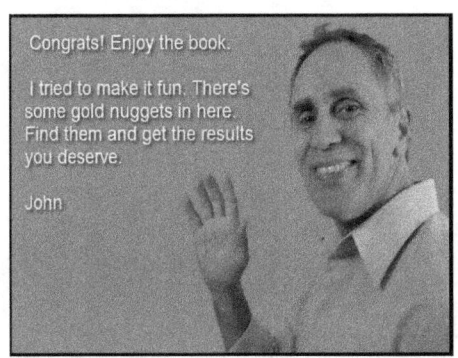

Congrats! Enjoy the book.

I tried to make it fun. There's some gold nuggets in here. Find them and get the results you deserve.

John

Firstly, thank you. I'm glad, no--scratch that from the record. I'm **thrilled**, you're giving me the privilege, to share dozens of my copywriting secrets (the real kind) with you. Take confidence, your time holds worth to me, and I'll stand on this promise: Your writing, whether personal or for profit, will in no sense of time, be the same.

Whether you're an email marketer, blogger or just a person who wants to impact your friends and family relationships, the principles of words on the brain--work the same.

Every thought we have or word we read, creates an electrical impulse. **Literally generating power in the brain**. The more brain regions that our words hit, the more neurons are energized. This creates deeper thought. The deeper the thought the more electrical impulses occur.

With each impulse, there is carried with it a corresponding biochemical component. These are what creates the emotions the reader feels. It works on everything you write. (Except maybe the grocery list) . This is where the title of the book came from Word-Power.

Maybe cultivating the relationships in your corporate clients through email would benefit you. Or, an author desiring more line weight in your story. How about a marketer, bent on crushing conversions, or a blog poster? Or just a devoted text-aholic and proud of it. Which ever of these are you, after experiencing this book -- *you will write the hell out of your copy.* "The End".

You'll never again write as you have in the past. Stack this on top of that--you'll never *read* copy as you have in the past. *Let's go!*

In just the past 10 or 15 years, technology allowed us to peer into the readers brain-- as they're reading! Using fMRI and other new realtime imaging technology. As a result, copywriting is changing forever.

Those secrets, now stand between the two covers of this book. And science itself demands their truth.

Writing covert copy. Influencing the readers mind with our words. Stealth mind hacks. Psychological principles and writing principles that create a **captivated reader or a motivated buyer**.

These writing secrets, or as I like to call them "Power Tweaks", literally **generate emotion**, in a reader. These power tweaks activate mental mechanisms and physical actions in readers. Literally generating power, through the increased neuron activity.

Every thought we have or word we read, creates and electrical impulse. The deeper the thought and more regions that are hit, the more electoral activity occurs. Each electrical impulse carries with it a biochemical component as well. These are what creates the emotions we feel.

Even more this emotion strengthens the personal bond, between writer and reader. Between two strangers. Dissolving that wall.

These copywriting secrets, enlist the autonomous functions of the human brain.

***

Prologue (About the book.)

This Word-Power book, leverages science, to interface our words to the mind of our reader. i.e. It'll hook you up. Sink a sharpened barbed hook, deep into warm gray matter of your reader's mind. That actually sounds kind of gross. I decided to leave it, for the questionable humor value it may add :-).

Word-Power writing secrets teach you a *second writing language*. Better put, it's the second half of your present writing language. The missing half for some. For most writers, it will *form a new writing style.* If you're a marketer, it could impact conversions. The reach capability of your message will be enhanced, to include the subconscious mind. This new writing style speaks directly and intentionally, to both left and right brain perception.

It sharpens the edge, of our present message, with cold hard science. Then balances and whets the blade, to sculpt a captivating message. One with literal dimension. Equips our copy, to penetrate the readers resistance, **with embedded overt and covert logic.**

These methods create a more compelling read, more engaging for the reader. These principles, can shape your message through a 3D like copy technique. Depth, feeling, sound, scent, motion will come to life in your readers brain. Using *neural sensory targeting or NST.* Engaging the reader on multidimensional levels.

In the short; bringing our copy to life. Experiential copy. That means the capability of touching your reader on both emotional, and intellectual levels. If you're a marketer, it means greater potential for conversion. To compel. If your an author, emailer or blogger, it means conveying not just your message,but **getting the reader to see, touch, feel and hear your message**. To believe your message. Our goal is to bring your message a bit closer to reality itself. Creating a virtual reality, *within your written words*.

Chapter after chapter is stuffed like a well bred turkey, on thanksgiving day, with full tasty aromatic details. Including research, studies, scientific tests, in depth explanations and commentary. Following each magnified chapter, I then **boil it down**, to an easy to remember phrase or two. Which I call the *Take-Aways*.

At the end of the book, is the *Take-Away* **Cheat Sheet**. It can be used like a quick-reference cheat sheet. Like a copywriting blue-print. To transform your content into neural targeted, compelling and converting copy.

This writing system is geared to increase _**your**_ personal knowledge. Your ability to connect more effectively, to anyone you write to. *You*, are the system. The principles can be applied to email marketing, blogs, ads, novels, emails and web pages.

No what kind of funnel you have, more effective copy can increase results.

How many times a day do you type a message? How many times will you type messages over the next 10 or 20 years? **How many people, may or may not be touched by your words**, over that time?

How many hearts, lives and relationships can you enhance over that time? And the people you touch, how will it affect their lives? How many lives will they affect? Has anyone in your life ever said or written something that impacted you? There's a lost at stake here. It's not just about writing or selling, it's about people, relationships and feelings. Okay, it's about selling. But it's also about knowing how to touch people with words whenever you want to. Communicating on a deeper level. It's about inspiring, compelling and helping others. It's about improving life.

It's this mental science of copy writing, that I found so fascinating. We all have amazing mental capability God has given us. Problem is we (including myself) don't usually tap into it. Our readers have this same capability. To perceive, in far deeper ways, that most writers address.

Our communication ability is miles greater than just letters from an alphabet. Human nature is fascinating. Analytics is fascinating. Writing is fascinating. The three together are thrice as fascinating. Okay, enough with the *fascinating*. It sounded real good the first time, but by the third pass it needed a little push :-).

The more I studied , researched and discovered how copy actually communicates unconsciously to the reader, the more unknown and unused these writing secrets seemed to be. That's the most exciting part. This era of writing, is a new era for writers. Scientifically speaking. It was impossible to know this stuff 10 or 20 years ago. Science hadn't discovered it yet. In fact, the technology to discover it, wasn't even invented yet. History is being made at this very moment in time. This book is the offspring to those discoveries.

An engagement level we dream our writing would reach, may not be possible, if we ignore the science of our readers brains. If we ignore what is actually occurring on a subconscious level, as our **carefully prepared copy greets a skeptical readers eyes**.

Don't be fooled, I'm definitely no scientist. Unless a science kit from my 1969 Christmas present counts:-) I still remember making "chocolate milk" from it, which you weren't supposed to drink. How dumb was that idea?

To break free from the limit's of *"me too"* writhing or ad copy styles. To engage or compel requires first *reaching our reader's mind*. Going beyond mediocre writing, might mean going beyond conventions of the past. Into a ***new age of writing***.

We all have that individuality, that want's to blow the bridges to convention. Rise above mediocre. NFL football star linebacker Ray Lewis. Who climbed from dirt poor, up to hero for man and kids. once said, *"No man should be content with being just basic"*. Who want's barely basic writing? I won't be a drone. Break free from the pack, take it to another level.

I want killer copy. Don't you? Content that *lives* in my reader's mind. Content that captivates. If you're ready - Let's drop the hammer on this party and ***Release the Copywriting Beast!***

***

One

Sick Skills.

First off let's clear some confusion up about me and this book. We're not here to teach you how to spell hippopotamus or when to use a adjective or noun. That's for your English teacher. I'd probably screw them both up anyway. I'm here to give you SICK SKILLS, not boring ones. Sick writing skills that you can't find ANYWHERE else. How to get your message into the mind of a reader, and believed. To persuade. That's what this book can do for you.

Writing copy in any form, is an <u>attempt to communicate our message</u>. Communication is based on two factors. **What we say, and what the reader thinks about what we say.** *If* they read it at all. Even getting the reader to read it is sometimes the challenge. The dilemma most of us writers and marketers collide with, is when those two factors; *what we say versus what the reader thinks about what we say* - conflict. The conflict occurs if the reader is taking in a different message or not appreciating the message, we are trying to say. When that occurs, they're not compelled and they won't engage. If you're a marketer or blogger, that's a big problem.

Part of that problem, occurs when our writing is sending an unintended message to their subconscious and a different literal message to their conscious mind. It's a *confused* message. We write with a dual language. Our left brain and right brain think on different terms and our conscious and subconscious do too.

For now, I can't risk throwing us off the present track with too much detail on that. So let's keep rolling, and we'll get to the detail soon enough. Trying to engage a reader or convert a prospect with a mixed message, will be a struggle. On the flip side. Copy that delivers a unified message, to both the conscious and subconscious minds, could be convincing and converting copy. When both left and right brain hemispheres are in agreement with your message, and both helping to convince the reader of your intended message, it's a powerful moment.

Getting people to believe what you're trying to say is a major factor in engaging them. Even in fiction, a "believable" concept is crucial. One method of measuring a writing concepts ability to impart belief, is to apply it to a sales offer. Some marketers run split tests to compare effectiveness of two different versions of a phrase. If more people are converted to buyers with one version over another, then we know which line was more convincing. More believable.

It's a way to measure belief and measure message penetration into the readers mind. If conversions increase, we know a message was more compelling. Authors and marketers are both doing the same thing. Selling. One's selling a story and the other is selling a product. Both need to be *convince* with words. Getting people to believe our writing is just as important as getting them to believe that a marketers offer is a good deal. For a reader to be captivated they must lend their belief to our story. Those are the scientific mind-hacking skills you're about to receive. 30 plus, chapters of classified copywriting assets.

Copywriting is changing course due to recent scientific discoveries into the human brain, and due to communication evolution in the world such as iPhones, e-mail etc. It might be a good time to do what I do. Grab a pen and a notebook for your favorite points. (FYI: you've just been brain-hacked, I'll explain later;-)

In this book I also put a concise couple of lines, after each critical principle. As a Cheat Sheet element. They're labeled *"Take-Aways"* **in bold.** Action plan specifics, at the end of each operational concept. You'll also find them listed at the end of the book, placed in a strategic order. For super easy print out. It's for converting everyday writing, into writing that cannot be put down.

The Action Plan becomes a handy writers tool pouch, for creating or editing standard copy into, high performance copy. Riding on your hip, you'll have most every tool needed to create killer copy.

My goal, is for you **to connect on both mind levels with your readers**. It's the only way to maximize your message. What ever your message may be. Whether it's a blog post, email conversation, mystery novel, business offer, web page, ad or children's book.

The easiest way to learn it, and to keep things in the most lethally compelling order, is to first lay a foundation. Why does it need a foundation? Because this particular *stuff* is new, fresh and understudied. Because we want to know *"why"* the car starts when you turn the key. Not just that it will start, but why it starts. True understanding.

When we were little pee wee shrimps, before we could write our own name, we first had to learn the alphabet. With that alphabet, we could then write anything we chose. Still, we're using that alphabet today, at this very ironic moment :-).

Discovery of the how and why. The logic behind it. I'll show you the *how,* which is the functionality. But also the *why*, which is the cause, mystery and discovery of it. If you're at all like myself, you'll want to understand *why* it works. Not just that it's supposed to. So you can actually believe it. And ultimately, be determined to put it to good use.

I'll show you how to engineer a compelling message, using research proven covert writing logic. I'll show you which elements breed a compelling message. How to load your copy, with neural-triggers. **See what prevents a message from being compelling. How to spot an ineffective mixed message.** How to build trust, right off the first swing of the bat. In your very first sentence even. What words and phrases trigger an emotional pull. Explore whether words can actually create physical action, or not. I'll show you what questions to ask, when to ask them, how to ask them, and why to ask them. I feel like I'm trying to cram a dump truck of content, into a paragraph, that only holds 8 ounces. It ain't gonna' fit ;-).

We'll discover how to engage our reader on two levels . That second perception level of writing, is the part usually missing from everyday writing. We'll see how to get the reader to ask you a question. Getting them to participate in a *conversation,* rather than just reading. Creating a two way internal exchange. How to get them to answer your question. How to get them to agree with you. How to get them to believe you. How to build momentum, culminating a dramatic moment that is felt. How to deliver emotional experience to your reader, and why you have to. You'll learn the proven science behind it all. Your copywriting, blogs, ads, books and email messages are going to another level. Starting **now**.

Two

Dual Perception--Writing that engages.

Every ad we write, email, blog post, book or web page we present is *__already__ transmitting a message on TWO levels*. Yep.

Though we type ONE message only, we send TWO. Like it or not, believe it or not. If you're writing to a human and you yourself are also in fact human, you're communicating on two levels. Conscious and subconscious levels. Don't freak out just yet...it get's pretty cool later. Basically, some refer to as right brain and left brain perception. Others don't associate right and left brain with conscious and subconscious.

More on that later. It doesn't really matter where they are located, as long as we agree they are different. I am sure, have already heard of it to some degree. **But have you heard of it in the concept of writing?**

I'll call these two levels of writing, **surface-copy and sub-copy.** *Surface* copy, is what most people focus on when writing copy. It's the literal presentation of words. Typically designed for rational thought. The explicit text. It's what our left brain (the language center) see's and interprets on the surface. Left brain typically specializes in facts. Language and math mainly. Our left brain reads using mostly that single type of language format. But our right brain hemisphere reads the exact same copy, using a different type of language format.

Left brain, reads visible copy. The Subconscious or right brain reads both visible and **invisible** copy. The *sub-copy*. More on invisible copy in just a tiny bit. Two brain hemispheres, two languages. The right brain is more like reader radar. It senses things, in a less literal way. It might perceive color, tone, context, emotion or other factors. Right brain looks at the big picture first. Left brain looks at the small pieces first. If you were talking to a person face to face, their expression, posture, body language, eye movement, speed of speech are the types of things the right brain would perceive.

For a writer, **ignoring either presentation could blur or even destroy**, our intended message. Our heart felt message, could fall right out of the clouds. And into the dirt. The person we're trying to move, isn't budged or touched in any way. Except maybe by boredom. Potentially creating a disconnection between writer and reader.

When our highest converting copy, and most engaging stories and messages become real to a reader, there's a reason why. Their mind has **chosen to receive it**. Which can only mean one thing. It's **communicating consistently on two levels**. The same two levels a person perceives real life with. Right brain and left brain perception. In synergy.

If that's how a reader is wired to think in real life, then shouldn't our concepts of writing , adapt to it? If yes, then how? Here's how; By including both levels of language in our writing. Both levels of perception in our message. *Surface copy and sub-copy*.

About those names. Surface-copy and sub-copy. Corny, I know, but I had to come up with fitting handles. Sub-copy I like. It's a well suited handle and makes perfect sense. Surface-copy, I'm not all that happy with, but it was better than "top-copy" so we're stuck with it. It doesn't matter what we call it. It only matters that we know it exist. Looking down at your keyboard, you'll see letters on top of the keys.

What you don't see on your keyboard, is the sub-copy that pressing those letters also creates. You cannot press one without the other. It's how humans communicate - two levels. Using two very different sides of the brain. See, we type our message on absolute terms. Literal terms. But the readers brain(s), reads and then interprets on both explicit and non-explicit levels. Here's what I mean..

A reader will consider not just what we type, but also what we DON'T type. If I type a message: *"I made $1,000,000,000 dollars, today"*. And that's all I type. What reader is going to believe that statement? Please tell me, I have a wonderful invisible car I just know they'd love to buy. Best part, it doesn't even use gas! Think of the dough they'd save ;). The answer: Nobody would believe that statement. Why?

How could they not believe it, if that's exactly what I typed? Two words. Right brain. Reader radar. Because the reader also perceives with the other side of their brain. The right side. Thank God. The right brain helped them understand the truth. It considers the fact that we didn't support our claim. B.S. alarms were flashing bright red strobes. Alarms are whaling at 90 decibels inside their head. It doesn't feel right. The right brain radar spotted that ill intentioned copy craft on the horizon, and proudly shot it down. Probably grinning as the message went into a tail spin. The defense system in their mind, alerted them that we are most likely not being honest in that message.

What's worse, is that now the right brain also picked up on our questionable values. Sensing less than forthright character. In reaction, they'll also now color everything else we type, with a yellow tone of caution. Because the first message proved to be exaggerated, the rest may be too. That's what they may think anyway.

So, the person reads what we type, but also what we don't type. Dual perception. One side of the brain reads the words, the other side reads or more accurately put, *perceives* everything else. Out of the two levels of copy we sent, they figured out the truth. The didn't just read what we wrote, they read what we didn't write too. Their two brain halves, are automatically helping them solve problems that may not add up. To protect them from the *"invisible car"* dealers of the world. C'mon, hey I was only kidding about that invisible car.....ummm it really does use gas. But, it's invisible gas and I sell that very cheap too!:-).

That $1,000,000,000 line, was just one obviously simple example, of how we are already using a dual language in our copy. Even if we don't know it. It's just one example, when in fact there are many aspects of copy, where two language levels apply. There were only 36 keystrokes in that $1,000,000,000 surface-copy sentence, but the reader's right brain added much more into the message. They read what we <u>did not even type</u>.

We *"whispered"* an invisible secret message to them, which stated the exact opposite of our typed message. A contradictory message, between the surface-copy and sub-copy. A mixed message. A confused message. Remember the right brain has it's own language format, and does not require text to be visible. It can fill in the blanks on it's own. Even large blanks. We sent a mixed message. Mixed messages don't convert readers into believers or buyers very well. Pulling the reader in, could be done easier when the dual language *we are always using*, agrees with each other.

Copy Cat

Imagine if you would, the most foolish thing you could possible say, in an ad or email message. Awe go on, it will be fun. Have you done it? Now imagine, you typed it in your offer or email just for fun, but did not send it. See, that wasn't bad was it? But then, your crazy neglected and bored cat, which you affectionately named *"Copy"*, wants your attention. So *Copy* (the cat) stepped on your keyboard, walking across it, insisting on your love. To your shock, and disbelief, the email offer was accidentally sent out by *Copy's* paws. Sent to all of your email list. Sent with the foolish, embarrassing copy you typed in **bold font**. That darn cat..

Moments barely pass, and that flood of embarrassment has now hit you like a tsunami. You're drowning in it. But it's too late. It's gone. To the readers. The message has been sent. Every embarrassing word being read. Everyone on your list is going to read it. Even as you consider this excruciating event, they've already commenced reading it. The end; of the imaginary story that is.

Now in that little blunder, which you will never, ever do in real life, is an analogy. Copywriters do this everyday, unknowingly, with their **<u>sub-copy.</u>** Oh mama. Whether we make a similar blunder with our surface-copy or our sub-copy, **there's really no difference to the reader**. Both ways can be picked up and understood, by the reader. Both do the same amount of damage.

Not knowing what our sub-copy is stating to the reader, can do the same damage as typing it outright in the surface copy. Right?

It's why, understanding how to communicate on both levels is critical for great writing. Dual perception writing is critical to move and touch people as you want to. The most engaging writing will hit both targets. Right and left brain perception. After all, if were not intentionally writing to the right brain, then were **unintentionally** writing to it. How can I say that? Well, unless we can flip a switch, to turn off the readers right side brain, like a light, then it's on. Right? (No pun :-) And if it's on, then that baby is going to work on your message. Righty is trying to help ole *lefty* out.

 If we only write to one side of the brain, and by that I mean only write to be read, rather than write to create experience, then isn't that what's happening? Our left brain **reads** words - our right brain **experiences** words. Over and over anew? Some words and phrasing are for literal purpose of rational thought, and others are experiential words and phrases. One delivers a **message** the other delivers the **experience** of the message.

Wrongly communicating to the left brain or to the right brain are both bad things. One level of miscommunication is just as convincing and damaging as the other. Great copywriters like yourself, consider **both levels of perception** all the time. In several more lines, I'll begin to explore the inner processing of the words in the readers brain.

Great writing is no less powerful than great movies. They both can translate a realistic message to our reader, all the way down to an unconscious experiential level.

By specifically targeting both brain regions in various ways, which we'll discuss, we can engage the reader strongly on both levels. Without them perceiving they've been mind-hacked. Hooking up your words to both sides of the readers brain. Converting our copy, into a reader-friendly copy. **Allowing the reader's mind to experience your writing in just the same way it experiences life itself.**

The specific words we choose, sentence structure, paragraph structure, emotional pre-framing, neural sensory targeting and many more specific tactics. All opportunities you can use, to determine how the readers brain is going to react to your copy. It's really easy to do, once the methods are out of the box.

I see little evidence that these concepts are being harvested by any majority of writers, yet. Science has only recently learned much of it. The *marriage* of copywriting and recent scientific advancements in reader thought, are only in the pre-dating stages.

By understanding in advance, what a reader responds to, on both levels, you'll know how their brain could react to your words. This gives you the opportunity to structure your message tactically. Allowing you to surgically tap into their thought center. Using your own neural targeted message. Hitting them on two levels. Right and left brain.

Even breaking it down into specific regions. For example consider these four versions of lines, which state the same thing, but in different ways.

I went to the store.

I cranked on the jams, latched my seat belt and cruised to the grocery store."

I cranked on the jams, latched my seat belt and cruised to the grocery store with my arm hanging out in the cool summer night air.

I clicked the stereo dial and was hit with a simultaneous smile-- my favorite tune just started! Pumping up the vibes, I had to cruise. This boring trip to the grocery store turned out alright after all. The rush of cool summer night air against my left arm stirred a scene in my brain, way back from my teenage nights. What a trip.

The first sentence did nothing for the right brain. All it did was deliver the left brain basics of the what happened. But is that one really all that happens when we go to the store?

Now the second, third and fourth were starting to engage it. I deliberately hit the senses in your brain. Used the sensory dimension of sound, temperature, motion, emotion and action. I still left out color, texture, taste, smell. Notice how much more real the lines *felt*, as they progressed? The idea is to engage the senses. Deliver experience. Not just tell the story, but show the story. Feel the story, hear the story, touch the story etc. In full sensory detail. **Just like reality.**

Hooking our copy up to their most influential brain regions, can harness persuasive mental and emotional leverage. Using both covert and overt language styles to do this.

Deploying just the right question as just the right time for example, can have specific effects on their curiosity, emotions, senses and on their desire to keep reading our message. It communicates our message on a deeper level. A double barreled approach to writing content. **Dual powered copy!**

Take-Away: Write copy for *both conscious and unconscious* levels of perception. Target both left and right brain awareness. More brain regions activated, means a more mentally engaged reader.

Three

The science of Engaging a reader.

There are 2 conversations going on, every time we communicate with anyone. On paper, email, web page, telephone or face to face. One conversation on the surface and the second conversation in the subconscious minds. By that I mean, the thoughts that happen automatically, behind the awareness of rational thought.

We have two brain halves. Seems sort of obvious to say, I know. What's easy to forget, is that our readers and prospects have two brain halves also. The two halves are barely even connected. Holding them in your hand, they'd almost look like two separate organs. No, I've never held one in person. Pass. But I have on video.

When you type the word *"cat"*, the reader's left side brain, identifies the word *"cat"* from stored history. Their right brain then creates images of *cats*. Then, the left side tries to recall a specific cat that you may have seen in the past. Then it projects an outcome into the future, based on all this information. That is how one brain scientist, described our two brain halves in action. The right side however performs even more.

Right brain handles the big picture. The environment, the setting, the mood, the tone, the colors, the feeling, the B.S. It also helps with images. It senses many different emotions. For a writer, this would equate to things like paragraph size, sentence length, headline intrigue, and the emotional pull or excitement of the story. Colors and sounds for example. It also picks up on a wide range of present emotions like greed, selfishness, generosity, love, caring, puffery, vanity, boastfulness, courage, fear, sorrow etc. Captivating a reader, means triggering those elements.

Each side thinks in different formats, left toward the front does the math and reading. Not that it matters where it's at, as long as we know it *is somewhere up there.* It thinks from past to future, in a linear path. Like 1, 2, 3, 4 etc. Right side only cares about right now, this moment. Instead of linear processing, it relies on parallel info processing. Not past to future, but joint side by side information. It sort of makes a bigger picture to help it understand the meanings of things. This awareness, of the <u>NOW experience</u>, is interpreted by our right brain and helps create feeling. It does this by creating hormones that then trigger biochemical reactions. Did you see that? Check your mirror. Tap the brakes. Pull over, to the *right*. Let's talk.

Check out what just happened. Boiled down, to it's core - **a <u>word</u> which we type into**

our copy, can create a biochemical change in another human being. That's sort of huge. We type a word, and little neurotransmitter peptides start ripping around their brain and body.

It changes the way they feel. It occurs largely through the right side of their brain. The electro-chemical action though, runs all over the brain and body and back to the brain again. This is what *YOUR* words can do! If you target the right side perception.

Now, maybe it's a good change, or a bad one. That part we haven't gotten to yet. What's my point? Your copy has the **power to change** the way people feel. No matter who you are, or where you came from, your words can change the way people feel. Throw it in first gear. Pop the clutch, and *smoke em*.. let's keep rolling..

Because each brain side thinks differently, they care about different things. They speak different languages. two languages. They see the same information, but in different ways. So, should our writing speak two languages as well? Or just one? I think two.

Four

Brain Ping Pong - Let's play!

Your serve. (There's a joke in there somewhere. About Four (the chapter) being for golf and not ping pong:)

Okay, so it's 4:02 A.M. and even waiting this long, wasn't easy. This idea I'm writing came to me, about one half way though my porcelain cup of decaf green tea, last night. Drank straight. Something I enjoy once every evening as I'm shutting down. In preparation for sleepy time. That stuff kicks in like a horse sized tranquilizer too. It could make a Clydesdale question his balance. Even with that weighting my eyes, I remained excited to get this analogy down in type. Before it got lost. Possibly forever. Lost in my not-totally-organized mind. So, finally, since this idea is obviously more important than sunrise itself, I'll lay it out for you.

There was something discovered many years ago, called the Stroop effect.

In fact, here's how it works. If you would type the work Yellow. Then change the font color of the word so it is Red in color the effect would occur. A reader would be urged by other parts of the brain to say Red as they read the word "Yellow". That's the Stroop effect. "The Stroop effect paper is one of the most cited papers in the history of experimental psychology." (Stroop, n.d.)

Named after the second guy to figure this out. The first dude was German I think, so I guess his name didn't count. Sort of of like Columbus discovering America--which Indians already populated. How come the Indians didn't get the credit? Why am I drifting off topic? My own mind, is being forced by my fingers, to type this pre-coffee message. It's wrong but my fingers are overpowering my brain, so what can I do?

The only thing I have in my system at this early hour is a 16 ounce glass of freshly squeezed lemon juice water. With bright yellow grated lemon peel for added benefit. So I'm drifting a bit. Hey, don't knock it till you've tried it. Not drifting, but lemon for wake up juice. I'm living proof, it's actually an energetic way to start the day. As you can tell.

So, the left brain would be urging them to say Yellow. But the red font color would trigger other parts of the brain to read it as "red". One word, but a mixed message. The battle of the brains. A neural paint ball match. **What it creates is interference in the reaction time of reading.** It hinders the reading and decision making process. Two conflicting messages, due to the two methods of brain perception. Left brain versus the visual color region processing. Some would argue, left brain versus right brain perception.

As you also know, the left and right brain sections interpret the world differently. They also process a message and a web page differently. They process the same information but separate ways. **Could your website be unwittingly creating the Stroop type effect?**

When a website visitor's eyes first enter your page, the right brain is the first on the scene. Colors, shapes and images are more quickly interpreted than text. So, even though you may have a loud textual headline on your website, **you also have an even louder Right brain headline**. The Right brain headline is seen first. It is made up of colors, images and shapes.

Right brain headline and Left brain headline. What this could mean, is that the Left brain textual headline is interpreted after the pre-frame, of the Right brain headline. If the Right brain imagery headline is conflicting with the Right brain textual headline then could we have the Stroop type effect?

It's two competing messages, based on two methods of perception. The Stroop effect is not just confusing, it actually stresses the visitor's brain. Dragging down the speed of their thoughts to interpret and make sense of the page. Those downsides clog up message flow, and conversion.

When readers eye-ball our copy, they are urged by both sides of their brain as they read. They experience our writing through this dual information stream. Urged to disagree in many situations, if the copy acts confused. Or if the page acts confused. Competing messages disrupt the thought process. **Optimizing a web page, is partly done by reducing the Stroop type effects.** The difference to the visitor's subconscious thought processing is like city traffic jam compared to highway travel.

There are two conversations going on at all time. If you're a marketer, it could be a deal breaker.

The reader cannot ignore either one. That's impossible. If we desire to reach into their readers mind and engage them, we have only one choice. To consider the dual language that the reader is by nature itself, forced to read with.

To accomplish this, we can empower our copy to speak two minds. In reality, we're **already** speaking to our reader on both levels. Whether we realize it or not. Copy that is not engineered to communicate on both levels, could have issues in engaging and compelling as intended. We still might be compelling, but maybe to do that opposite decision that we set out do.

A reader cannot disable the right side of their brain. Again, there's only one solution. To deliberately send a consistent message to both hemispheres of the brain.

In tests of direct mail, fine stationary and opulent presentation converted less than standard. Why? Right brain perceives the attempt to impress the reader with something other than the offer or the merit. The right brain may cut through the camouflage, distinguishing spectacle from truth. Alerting the reader as a watchful sentry, recalling cautious emotions. The triggered emotions put the reader on guard. The embellished presentation, suggests to the right brain, an attempt to <u>sell</u>. Rather than an attempt to <u>provide</u>. Presentation is read first by the right side. Facts matter to the left side.

Take Away: The readers *right brain radar* will bust mixed or confused messages.

Compelling copy should speak the same message on both perception levels.

Oh Baby!

When we're born, the fastest part of our brain development is our right brain, which some think houses our subconscious. According to the American Journal of Neuroradioligy our right hippocampus, grows faster than the left hippocampus 91% of the time during the first 2 years. The hippocampus part of the brain does stuff like, emotions and senses. Things such as smell, tones and sound. My hippocamus feels smarter just typing that big ole word. It connects them with memories. So when we're babies, the right brain is growing faster. What is it your cute smelling little babies loved to do?

Them little cuddle bugs love to look at your face and listen to your voice, right? All powdered up and ready for the day's barrage of incoming kisses. Watching your face and eyes, sensing tone and touches.

It's our first language! We sense love and fear right away as babies. Those aren't words to a baby, they're feelings. Right brain feelings. Language and logic however, are slower to develop. The reason I mentioned this, is to emphasize the primary roll that the right side of our brain plays in our life. Starting from the time we were first born.

It's why babies can be so happy and laugh - for no apparent reason at all. They speak and perceive with the love and emotions they sense and see. It's their first language. Our first language too. A smile, a touch, a funny face, communicates very clearly to them.

It's the right brain language they speak. Creative type writing, and marketers need to speak that same language at times. That sense we were born with, never changes. For a writer to not speak that language, is to not speak our very first language. It's also why they say dogs can smell fear. Animals use this type of brain function to read each other, and to read us. Cesar Millan the dog whisperer guy, is a master at using body language to communicate with them. The language is very real, and even prevalent in nature.

People that have had strokes on their left side, are said to often still able to perceive what is being said, even though the language part of their left brain is no longer working. It's through this *awareness* part of the right brain that it occurs. Expressions, tone, posture, gentleness of touch, speed or abruptness of movement, all convey a very clear sense to our right brain. This has been proven by a well known scientist, in an unexpected way. Through interviews and videos she's shared things that some have said, changed their lives. Her name is Jill Taylor.

Five

Brain Doctor has a Stroke - see's it all from the INSIDE...

February 8, 2008, Jill Taylor walked steadily onto a stage in Monterey California. It was a TED conference, where inspiring stories are often told. The video recordings of TED are then made available to the public. They're found on youtube. (Taylor 2008) On the video, Jill shared that because of having a brother diagnosed with a mental illness, she felt led to choose a career path of a brain scientist. She trained at Harvard. The bizarre story she was about to share, wasn't one she chose, but one that chose her.

From her mind blowing experience in 1996, Jill was able to break new ground in her field. It occurred as a result of a blood vessel exploding on the left side of her brain. She was hit with a massive stroke. The TED conference stage, is where she was about to share that fateful moment-by-moment account.

Due to her training, she was able to recall the experience in great detail after she recovered. As a brain scientist, witnessing a stroke from the INSIDE as her brain was shutting down, was a lesson that books could have never taught her.

Little does the audience know she's about to whip out a real human brain. The dangling spinal cord still attached, as she casually holds it up in her hands. That's what I call good prop. As disgusting as that sounds, there is a reason I described it.

As she held the two brain halves up, it's very clear that they were almost completely separate. Right and left. Very little brain matter joined them together. It doesn't appear so much like a single organ. **It looks more like two separate organs**.

My point? Writing which only address one side of the brain, is missing one half of it's target.

What makes Jill's story incredibly valuable, even for writers or marketers is that she spent those early post stroke days, with the left side of her brain disabled. Took her eight years to recover. Relying almost exclusively on her right side brain, in her early stages.

Think about what this implies. Our left side brain is our language side. So how will she communicate herself to others? How would she be able to interpret others communications? How will she explain that she is having a stroke? How will anyone understand what she is trying to tell them, when she cannot talk? How will she perceive her own reality? How will her reality change? Her single experience reveals beaming clues about the power of the right brain.

Jill's story transparently reveals the source of untapped power, in our second level of thinking. She uncovers the ability to negotiate her new life while recovering, using predominately the right side of her brain. The same thought station that we sometimes dismiss or ignore as we write our copy.

TIME Magazine chose Jill, as one of the 100 Most Influential People in the World, for the year 2008 (Clark 2008). Her book is a great investment to any copywriter. She's also been interviewed on Oprah, and other printed interviews.

During this life changing stroke in the early stages, she could not walk, talk, read, write, or recall anything in her life. Jill said at TED on video, she was reduced to the brain status of an infant.

Yet that infant mind, could sense, good nurses from those certain not so caring nurses, which made her fearful. She could understand what someone meant, without understanding their words. It was communication on a different level. Not on a dialect level, but on an experiential level. The reason I watched her video in the first place is because of a relative in my own family that had neurological challenges.

Left brain is an observer, the right brain is a participant. They learn in different ways, and so our writing should address them in different ways. Think of the untapped potential of copy that doesn't presently speak the correct message to one half of their readers brain. For an email marketer, fixing that, is like doubling your mailing list overnight! Okay, slightly overemphasized, but the point remains valid, and still kicks butt. Right?.

Her New York Times bestselling memoir *My Stroke of Insight: A Brain Scientist's Personal Journey* was published in 2009 by Viking Penguin. Her website is "mystrokeofinsight", if you care to get it. Highly recommended.(Taylor 2009)

Understanding how our readers mind works, helps us write more compelling copy. More compelling copy increases conversions and even better, touches the hearts and minds of our readers.

Six

My interest in the readers mind....a personal story.

This subject of the non-logical part of our brain, is more than just book knowledge to me. Not that I have book knowledge. It came partly from a place of personal experience with a loved one. Born with a special purpose in life. A life that was filled with challenges. Jill's story helped me discover how to communicate without words. To communicate that you love them, and to know with certainty that they might feel that. I'm grateful to her for that.

We communicate on two levels. Not one.

And, the most powerful level, is not our language center. Instinctively our first level of communication, is largely through the right brain. The two sides work together, but in different ways.

Anyone can type a message. Getting our message from the screen into a readers brain, requires them to let us in. They must truly believe and even be moved emotionally toward us. Then the message will lift off of the screen and be allowed into their mind, engaging them.

Seven

The Building Blocks of Legendary Copy

Fact or Fiction?

March 17, 2012 New York Times published a story. *"Your brain on fiction"*. In the article, Annie Paul reported on a study and a strange neurological fact. One that was only recently discovered. (Paul 2012)

When we hear various *"facts"*, a certain region of our brain is activated. The Broca's area. I've got no idea what a friggin' broca is, but you got one. You're reading these words with it. Or you can just call it the front left part. The language processing center.

With facts, our brain pretty much limits it's signals to that part. However....scientist recently learned that our brain works differently for **stories.**

Stories that are real, or fiction. Doesn't matter. For stories, our brain engages many other parts of the brain. Left side and right side. Both are stimulated. The exact sub-region it activates, depends on the exact words it encounters. Now, that last sentence is sort of notable. **Different words activate different brain regions**. That lil' fact, is a crucial building block for marketers or creative writers. Any copywriter really. It will be spotlighted in great detail, but for now just don't let it slip away.

What it means for a copywriter is this: Words can be dispatched, to target specific regions in the brain. Activating neurons in those areas. These regions include sensory triggers. **Neural sensory targeting (NST),** is the deliberate targeting of specific brain regions using words.

Neural sensory targeting. What occurs after those regions are *hit* with words, will be covered later. The key point now, is that specific words are directed to, and received by, distinct parts of the brain. Not many years ago, copywriters did not have this information. It was only recently discovered.

Scent related words like lavender, pepper, or coffee, would trigger a response from parts of the brain that deal with smells. Lets test that theory out. now.. **Starbucks!** You smell coffee? No? Oh well. Maybe it's my wife making a pot. Back to the research..

When shown other words such as *"key"*, and *"chair"* which didn't relate to smells or taste, those *smelly* regions of the brain, did not show response. Did you see that? Brakes on. Put it in park. Time for a chat. Okay, this is truly no small matter. Let's just make sure we're cooking in the pot here.

Take-Away: *Different words* cause our brain to react in different regions, depending on the words. The words we choose to write, are sent to different places in the readers brain. Determined by the exact word chosen. This knowledge, gives us incredible power. Power to deliberately *target* specific brain regions with our words. *NST or Neural Sensory Targeting.*

Reading simulated reality.

A New York Times article stated, that a novelist and University of Toronto professor, Keith Oatley, proposed that **"reading produces a vivid simulation of reality."** (cited in Paul 2012)

If you've ever read one of the best selling David Baldacci books such as the fantasy novel *"The Finisher"(2014)*, you'd find it hard to disagree. Writing done well, is a vivid reader experience. This dude lays down lines. He does with a pen, what a seasoned Ninja can perform with a sword. Selling over 100 million books, counting all of his titles, proves one thing. People love words when they're put together well. But doesn't that also beg on knee and heel, one more slightly overlooked question? Why?

Why, do readers love words, that are put together well? It's a larger question. Hinting at an overall driving force. What is it, that readers are experiencing, which makes them want to read all those millions of books? Inside their head, what is occurring, that they want more of? For now, we'll just say - something is occurring. It has to be, or they wouldn't be forking out green paper for white paper. Right? The finer details of what is happening is of major consequence for copywriters. That's why I covered it in such detail in the upcoming pages. Just keep it in mind as the chapters come together - something is occurring that makes readers, want to keep reading.

3D Copy

Multidimensional, neural sensory targeting

In that laboratory study which Annie reported on, certain scent related *words* activated the same parts of the brain as as the physical aroma itself. The same parts used when we literally smell, (not in the *"you stink"* sense, but in the "*that cookie smells good*" sense). When we smell a hot baked oatmeal cookie for instance, a certain part of our brain get's busy. What does it do? Interprets those smells for one thing. They're sent to it from our chemoreceptors (Basically, your nose dude....read a book.... oh, you are? sorry:-). As you can already tell my true gift is clearly a comedian, but I'll try to restrain myself. Hey, I'm a right brain thinker what can I say?

Those smells are turned into electrical signals. Then our brain gets em and interprets the smell's signals. Now is when the magic starts to happen. Because it's sent to more than one place. The parts of our brain that receive this info, is the limbic system- stay with me now! Our Limbic system includes a few brain sections. Including the hippocampus, and the amygdala. Sections linked to our **memory and emotions**.

Almonds and National Security.

The amygdala is the size of an almond. Which is why they named it a word that means almond. One in each half of your brain. The emotional power of the amygdala is something you're happy to have on your side. This is the part of the brain that can make a Navy Seal tap out. Literally. And we know, them dudes don't play. They call it, the emotional command center for our brain. (Green 2012)

N fact, Navy Seals have to go through specialized training to learn to override their amygdala's control of their decision making process.

During high stress scenarios our emotions instinctively override rational thought. As a self preservation mechanism. Learning to replace fear with rational thought is their goal. Like when their brain is telling them they're probably going to die if they don't come up for air. They do it in San Diego California, at the Navy Seals Special Warfare Command Center.

It's like anti-fear training, where they are trained to think rationally in the face of their most primal fears. (Disclaimer: Navy Seals are legendary. I am no Navy Seal, and have no Seal training or association with them. My knowledge is strictly from public research material.) Learning to push beyond fear and regaining rational thought, under extreme life threatening pressure, is obviously part of what makes a Seal a Seal. Unbreakable courage like that, puts the "F" in Freedom. It's partly why they're able to stand up to fear in the field--and then walk straight through it.

The amygdala is said to be one of the most interconnected parts of our brain. What's interesting, is the the signals reach this emotional command center, at double the speed compared reaching the frontal lobes (the rational thought region). Why is that important for copywriters? Emotions kick in, before rational thought does. Nice.

The brain prioritizes emotions over rationale. Could be why people enveloped in love do some ca-razy things, ya think?

All that was said to lay ground work. In the case you wanted to grasp clearly where these scent signals, are being sent. (No pun.) So these scent signals are ultimately traveling to an emotional powerhouse, in the brain. A group of brain regions comprised partly by the amygdala and hippocampus. This group is the region we just learned about, the *limbic* system. It's job? Translating sensory data. Part of that data, is words. The type we can transmit in our copy. **It is directly hitched to our experiences, within our personal history.** Linking our emotions and memory. You did it! We made it through the weird words part. Fiver!

Glad that's over with. That's why, when you smell a certain food, it may instantly bring with it, a cherished childhood memory. (Or a bad dinner experience at Aunt Bitsy's:) Or, your eyes may cloud suddenly with a tear, from some long buried thought of a past moment in time. Involuntarily pulling you through a time warp, to some tender crack in time of your emotional history. We can hit those same regions with words.

Those scent brain regions carry out two related actions. They produce what we wind up smelling, but also create an emotional response to the smells. A scent response which was hardwired to our memory. That's kinda huge.

Huge enough that the brain rolls out a princely red carpet for our scent words arrival. They're fast-tracked. Launching us backwards in time, and doing so in less than a second.

Studies show our triggered response to smells, occurs faster than to sight or sound. All said, it's one influential sense. By introducing word *scent* triggers, we gain direct access to the readers memory and emotions. Infusing our message with their life experiences to some degree.

In the deaf and blind community, smell becomes a heightened sense. Their brain does this to compensate. Its' used to identify people, locations, tasks, and other descriptive aspects of every day life. People working with kids facing these challenges, are encouraged to wear the same perfume or cologne every day. It's so the child without sight can recognize who is working with them. Holding tooth paste or soap near their nose, signals to them in a subtle way, what it is time to do. So they're not startled or uneasy about what could be happening to them. My point?

People use their sense of smell as an identifier. A link to memories, experiences and emotions. It's trusted. Smells carry with them, internalized personal associations. What does that mean for a copywriter? Using words that stimulate those brain regions, can call to mind experiences, sensational memories and emotions. It's an association opportunity, which can be introduced through copy. These are neural sensory trigger points. We have the power in our words, to recall and create feeling in a reader.

In the winter of 2007, a paper was published at Meikai University. (Toshiko 2007) This study of aromatherapy arrived at some conclusions. That the smell of Lavender and Rosemary reduced cortisol levels in the participants. Cortisol is a hormone that our body creates, to deal with stress. Commonly referred to as the stress hormone. It does bad things when out of balance. Some animals die from lack of it, some people have shortened lives from too much of it. It's purpose is to aid us in a temporary threatening *fight or flight* situation.

To jack us up. Prolonged stressful situations however, build up this unhealthy cortisol hormone level. In the short - without a fight to burn it off, it's stored. It derails many bio-processes in our body when accumulated. Also makes belly fat. Divorce, financial

29

struggle, job pressure are some examples of prolonged stress that can build up cortisol levels. It deteriorates physical and emotional health if we sustain high cortisol levels. The fact that scent has been proven to counteract stress, is meaningful from an emotional perspective. Emotions and hormone balance are directly linked.

Through several studies, aromatherapy has been shown to stimulate many positive physical, mental and emotional reactions. Even diseases such as Alzheimer's have shown positive cognitive results from it. It produces a similar affect as green tea or dark cocoa. They declare war on free radicals. Free radicals act like the poisonous exhaust products left over from our body creating energy. Let's keep waxing on. The reason I bring this up, lies in the next paragraph. After you.

Lemon, rosemary, lavender, peppermint, rose and orange are used for at least three things. Anxiety, stress and depression. The effect of scent on emotions, memories and even physical and mental health, gives us some idea, **how those related brain regions can impact our readers**. If and when they're activated. By including this breed of sensory triggers in our copy, we're stimulating the reader. Adding more sensory dimension to the message. They would be scent, emotions and personal history. Enlivening our message with a sensory quality that can be experienced. That trait is an aspect of reality. Bringing our words closer to reality, in the readers mind.

What is it that makes the physical world feel and look real to us? Isn't it our confirmed senses? Color, depth, texture, scent, sound and motion and taste. Even memory is a sense, because time itself is perceived by history. Sensing motion also requires sensing time. So, if reality is determined by our confirmed senses, and a copywriter can trigger those senses, doesn't our message gain traction?

Does our message become more real? More believable? Don't answer yet, because you may be thinking this: "It can't be real to the reader if it's just a word. It it's just a word it's not physically real."

Okay, well then can you answer this question: Have you ever had a dream where you were in water, such as swimming or in the rain, or maybe spilling something on yourself in the dream? While you were inside your dream world, did it seem real to you? Did you feel wet? Has a dream ever felt real to you? If your answer is yes, then that proves our brain can indeed make a thought take on aspects of realty. **All the way to the point of us believing they are entirely real.**

It would not help if I get too far off track here, so let's just put that on the back burner for now. There's more on it to come still. Before we put the lid back on though, there is one more question that's not yet been answered.

Remember the *larger* question?

Think back, to the beginning of this chapter. Remember the question about why readers buy millions of books? The question about, what is a reader experiencing when they read, to make them want to keep buying books? This question here -*What is it, that readers are experiencing, which makes them want to read all those millions of books? Inside their head, what is occurring, that they want more of?* Is it possible that we just uncovered at least part of that answer? Good copy that creates dimension, might be delivering a sense of reality. One they could be experiencing as they read.

So by adding scent triggers, we are more fully addressing the multi-sensory mind of our reader. What we experience in a multi-dimensional way, is harder to deny. Because reality itself is multi-dimensional.

The more sensory brain regions we trigger, the more dimension our copy projects. We can't deny what we have experienced.

It's what makes up our beliefs. Dimensional copy is believable copy. If the reader can see it, hear it, feel it, smell it, they are more likely to believe it. We usually try to remain consistent with our beliefs.

Targeted sensory words and phrases to these regions, arrive on a subconscious level. Undetected. It covertly adds emotional and historical depth to our copy. Historical because our readers memory and emotions are triggered, and they are rooted in history. Believability may be naturally enhanced, using multi-sensory targeted copy. It also may be kicking the fun-meter up a few notches for the reader.

Our brain generates the smell and generates emotional memories, from that physical scent we take in. Our brain, creates the smell from the info the nose delivered. Well targeted sensory words can do a similar thing. (but a real cookie still taste better than a word...especially with Starbucks;-)

Here's my point. A **word** can, activate the same region of brain that a freshly baked soft golden brown around the edges oatmeal cookie activates! Sheesh, that's a lot of words for a simple point. Why didn't I just say that to begin with? Because I wanted you to grasp WHY it works too. Let's get back to Annie and cookies..;-) Yum!

Take Away- *Scent.* The word "cookie", activates the same part of the brain as a real cookie. *Scent* related copy does two things. Creates a present sensory experience, and recalls emotional memories connected to those scents. It adds emotional, historical and sensory dimension to our copy. Enriching reader experience. Making our copy more believable.

Take-Away: Using scent related words, activates emotions. Emotions are processed faster and stored longer, increasing retention of our copy.

The study Annie reported on was performed in Spain. It was published in the NeuroImage journal in 2006. They used brain scans. When regions of our brain become active, blood pumps oxygen to that specific region. When blood is carrying oxygen it has different magnetic properties. This is what the MRI scanners measure. Thinking neurons receive oxygen rich blood at a greater rate than inactive neurons. This measurement principle is also applied to create cutting edge (i.e. Cool) technologies .

Color of scent (how to pump up the scent).

How about splash of color? Let's apply another brain asset, by attaching *association*. Association relies on memory and past connections to link things together. The wielding of color words (not referring to colored words as in font color, but words such as "*bright yellow*", or "*deep red*" or "*purple*") which correspond to the scent related message, grows another dimension into our message. Another aspect of everyday reality, is color. By painting our message, we intensify it to another level. Again, boosting the dimensional aspect of our copy. Giving the scent message a corresponding color. Or giving the color a scent.

Example if I mention the scent of lemon in a message, then I should also mention the color of bright yellow. It's called the *color of scent.* Proven in laboratory multisensory studies was a powerful link. A link that actually enhanced the smell and taste of things. For these tests they used brain scanners (fMRI). When pairing color with it's associated scent or taste, a profound effect occurred. Get ready for a stretched out word.

Back up a bit. One more step. That's good. Hold the door for me.. Okay, here it comes ... It was called a Neurophysiological correlation. (Yea, I'm sure I'll use that word again...not). In you and me terms, it just means what we see visually, affects what we *smell* and what we *taste*. In a significant way too. Visual influences, interact with our olfactory nerves (our smellers'). **Colors influence smells**. Cool huh? (Told you I'd toss some cool stuff in. :)

What I'm pointing out, is how to make the scent copy more effective--by also using color words with it. Olfactory nerves just transfer the smells to our brain, basically. They start right in between your eyes and run straight on up, into the ole noggin. Have you heard the common chef's adage: *"Presentation is 50% of the dish."*? Well this here scientific study, just proved that adage is material scientific fact.

Are you a wine taster? I'm not, but I sure drank more than my share of it. Not lately, but back when cars, cruising and partying appeared more promising than working. Found out later in life, that wasn't exactly the case. If you are (a taster) then you know how the wine connoisseurs, hold that crystal glass up to the light and then to their nose. For color and scent evaluation. I've always secretly wanted to do that, but I wouldn't really know what I was looking for. It all looks good to me:-).

Their *scent* reviews during testing showed they were "dramatically influenced" by the *colors* they saw in the wine. Color influenced scent. It was part of the study. (Don't know much about wine, bu I am an excellent coffee connoisseur. Colors, scent, and temp all get me happy on my coffee trips). Their conclusion: Colors influence our scent perception. Dramatically. As they do with taste as well. A bright red strawberry drink smelled more pleasant than when they colored the same drink green. It makes sense when you think about it. We sort of expect a certain flavor or scent from a specific color.

Like a brown banana or a happy yellow one. I know which of the two I'd reach for. How about a green banana, would you look forward to biting into that? Not me. My expectation of sweetness and softness would be leaping out of the window. That good ole banana flavor wouldn't be calling my name.

Before I ever tasted it, I would come to that conclusion. Wouldn't you? Our brain obviously is trained to associate the two together, color and taste. Or color and smell. Consider this. Our entire life's experiences might have trained our brain to associate them together. To help us. If your brain is trained that way and mine, then we could make a large bet, the readers is too. What profit does this knowledge give to a writer of copy, a blogger, author or serial email writer?

Well, adding a color reference to our scent related words heightens the effect of both. Stronger copy. More intense. More believable. More real. More emotional pull. More memories drawn up. A better reader experience. More life like copy. Greater retention. More engaged reader. More hungry reader (I made that last one up:) More sensory dimension in the message. **A more believable and reactive statement is molded, using both color and scent matching references.**

One shade closer to reality.

As you know, color is *"constructed"* in the brain. It's not actually seen with the eyes. Our brain generates the color we are visualizing. *Words* such as "red", "blue", "turquoise" and my personal favorite "coffee" etc. strike a direct hit, to the same room in the brain, as *seeing* the actual colors themselves. The electro-chemical signals wind up in the same place. They activate the same neurons.

So. steady your piece, and shoot a paint ball into your readers brain, by using color words. Here's what happens when you do.

The color signals are more like a machine gun or a shot gun. Here's why I say that. They take parallel paths, hitting multiple places in the brain such as motion, texture and shape regions. At least according to the trusty Harvard University Gazette. One shot of color hit's multiple sensory regions. Lot's of bang for the buck.

Take Away: *Color words* (red, blue, yellow etc.) activate the same multiple parts of the brain as seeing the color itself.

On the opposite foot, matching the wrong color reference with a scent reference would reduce the impact of both. That's a bad thing. Get ready for a long sentence. Take a deep breath first. Okay, go. That is to say, the emotional, experiential and personal historical relevance that our words have on the reader, will be reduced or enhanced, depending on how well we match the color and scent wordage in our copy. Let it out, just let it out.

Let's continue. Paired building blocks like this, set apart great copy from everyday copy. Color and scent are powerful mind grabbing tools for content writers.

One 65 year old color blind artist, was disgusted by the grayish dead appearance of his food he was eating. His tomato juice was reportedly black to him. He had to do something about it. So he switched to mostly black and white food. My point? Color means a lot to our brain.

Don't know about you, but I think this is pretty cool stuff. The test subjects were scanned while they were given the smells and colors separately and again when given in paired combinations. Their reactions *"increased progressively"* the more corresponding the color-scent match became. (Österbauer 2005)

Color cues impact scent and response. The study was published in the Journal of Neurophysiology in the summer of 2005. (Darn, I didn't plan on ever using that word again..sorry bout that. It's the last time, I promise:-). That chapter was a pain, I know, but the color-scent concept can give our copy some emotional punch.

Take-Away: *Activate more* reader brain regions, to engage the reader. Do it by inserting *sensory rich words*. Compliment scent related copy with their associated color words, to intensify the impact of both. *Taste* suited color words, also intensify *taste* related messages. Targeting multiple senses, creates multidimensional copy.

Take-Away: *Wrong color matching*, (mismatched color to scent or taste) detracts from the neural intensity of both.

Eight

Seeing thought and steering by thinking.

"Seeing thought" and *"Steering by Thinking...?"*

Steering by thinking, hmmm? Maybe that was the maniac in front of me on the highway yesterday...naahh.

If you think the accuracy of this type of research is unreliable, think again. (with the left side) Okay admit it, that one was almost funny...

These same type of fMRI scanners used in the studies, have been tested as lie detectors and have scored between 76% to over 90% accurate. In fact, brain imaging is so accurate that a company (Emotiv), was able to build a headset that does something unusual. We might call it the lazy man's remote control. That head gear allows us to remote control a device, by *thinking*. Mind reading technology is in no way coming, it's here.

The ability to "see thought", is at the door. Wheel chairs, can now be guided by thought. These products have already hit the market. Not exclusively for the super rich either. They cost under $1000.00. Here's a scary off topic thought. Could they make a "thought remote control" to fire a gun? Yikes.

"Eye Touching"....(eeewww.....huh?)

What happens once the information of a typed word, is passed to the readers eyes? Let me rephrase that. What happens when people read a word?

Is it mental or is it a physical experience? When we touch an object with our finger, our brain reacts with a response from the *"touch"* territory in our brain. We then are granted a physical sensation of the object from the nerve response. But what if we just see a **word** such as "sharp", which relates to touching an object? Rather than actually touching the physical object. How does our brain respond to that "word" object?

Nine

Words versus Reality, inside a readers brain...

You buckled up..?

March 25 2008, Emory University, reported research on these lines. The big question is; how real does it get? Will our brain just see the *"text object"* like any other form of text word? Could this touch word receive unique neural routing? Or would it be treated plainly, like non-touch words? Remember this taunt from when we were kids? "*Sticks and stones can break my bones, but* **words** *can never hurt me*". Is that phrase factual, or not? Would the word "sharp" actually be sent somewhere different in the brain, because it's referring to a "*sharp*" touchable object? Here's what happened.

People that read words relating to touch, showed response in touch related parts of the brain. The same part of the brain that is activated when we physically touch a [sharp] object. What does that mean for a copywriter? If we use the word "sharp" the reader experience a thought in the same part of the brain as if they physically touch a sharp object. That's not to say it a a conscious thought or unconscious thought, but it is a thought. Both have influence on the reader.

Unfortunately the words "sticks" and "stones" were not tested and were beyond the scope of this investigation. It figures right? Probably the people doing the study, were the same ones yelling the bad words about me as a kid! No wonder they didn't want "sticks and stones'" tested.

The neural imaging was done with fMRI brain scans as the test subjects were reading.

What does this mean for a copywriter? The words we type, are categorized by the brain. Different categories are sent to different places. Some touch words are sent to the same place in the brain, as signals from physically touching an object. That's *heavy*. Did you feel that?

Words about motion, triggered brain regions that ordinarily process physical motion. Hmmm...I think my chair just moved when I typed that....I told you to buckle up:). It was a fairly extensive study. The end of the point is this -- **Our brain doesn't draft much distinction between <u>words</u> <u>read</u> and experiencing the real thing**. Solid. Great news for writers huh?

Still, that sounds a bit much doesn't it? I mean does it really ring true in your right brain? The B.S. meter? Are there circumstances where this would not work? Or does it work all of the time? Would the results change, depending on the reader, or even the readers state of mind? Such as where they were or what was around them, while reading those words?

Here's the difference.

The significant difference that I see, is that the readers environment keeps the reader in balance with that environment. I would assume the right brain plays a big role in that. The reason why I believe that, is because our brain is also processing other information at the same time we are reading that text object word. It's processing data from our other senses at the same time we're reading the words. Here's how it could work.

For example: Let us blindly imagine - You're lying contently on your family room couch. It's a warm Sunday afternoon. Ball game playing on the TV, which is turned down low. In your relaxed right hand sits a well written book. This book tells the story of a person, much like yourself, only that this person was bitten by a venomous striped snake. Bit while camping in the Canadian forest. You're reading that book, while laying on your soft couch and feeling the warm sun beaming through the window. The bright sun also illuminating the very book you are enjoying. Somebody must have scored in the game, because the crowd on T.V. just picked up in volume. Take about 5 or 10 seconds to sense how you would feel about that snake story during your read. So here's what's happening in your brain.

In your family room, the household environment is counteracting much of the sensations that the words in the book are feeding to your brain. Outside a lawn mower sounds off, being pushed back and forth. A car passing by in a hurry, gives off another sound. Kids in the back room talking about who's turn it is. Sounds, smells, surroundings and familiar comforts are also feeding information to your brain, at the same time your reading the book about the snake. Counteracting the power of the books story. Gathering this wide assortment of data, the right brain is very much aware of it's surroundings. It helps balance what the left brain is reading. Remember the right brain is your B.S. meter. Reader Radar. So in your family room, you're not feeling all that concerned about snakes biting you. Does that sound close to correct? Now let's spin it around and switch it up. Snap out of that scenario, grab a few essentials, because we're taking a trip.

Believe in a different land.

The comforts in your home, that unroll your stressful days, are now parked hundreds of miles behind. Visualize a changed environment. A natural domain. You're not anywhere near home sweet home, or even in the same state. Besides that, a change in climate has swept in, with a discomforting cool dampness. In this fantasy you're reading through that same *"Venomous Viper Bites Camper"* book.

Only this time you're not on your soft couch reading it. That ball game was two days ago. Instead you're sitting, in a tent. And can't quite find satisfaction in your comfortless ground level position. Squirming away from the rigid lump under butt. Negotiating a compromise with the hard ground, seems to be a losing case. So you lay on your side, propping your head up with one hand. Against your cheek. *Finally.*

There is still one matter, which hasn't changed. The book. You're reading through those identical pages. Same book, same letters--about the same venomous striped snake. Only this time it's being read from inside your small green nylon tent. Just feet away from a forest. It starts getting a little to dim after thirty minutes of the story, so you seal it. The breeze is giving the sides of the tent a noisy shaking. A tent perhaps half your age. It's a solo trip, you're all alone, and are intently aware of that. A windy sunset is arriving at your camp site. Keeping warm should be no problem though, because siting nearby is a large pile of sticks.

From the untouched shape of that stick pile, it seems to have been here for a season or two. It lays heaping, no more than three feet away from the edge of the tent. It's to the left side. The right side, leads down to a half dried overgrown creek, which feeds the lake. Behind the tent, is an unsegregated population of trees. Going back further than your sight.

So here you are. Next to a pristine lake in the Canadian forest.. Dusk is here with you, so it's time to think about pacing a few steps over to the large tangled wood pile because it's about time to start that fire. Isn't that where *snakes* are known to veil themselves? In wood piles? In the lowered lighting, your eye scopes each branch two or three times, over it's length. Just to be sure it is in fact a stick your hand greets. At the same time before grasping each one, your panning the entire pile, for any possible movement. Some friendly human company would be welcomed right about now. Out here, your neighbors have four legs or wings...or maybe ...no legs at all!

Take a few long seconds to grasp how your slivering snake concerns, would crawl through your mind, and weigh on your thoughts differently there. From the same book. See the difference?

Here's what the NY Times put in print, during the early spring of 2012. "What scientists have come to realize in the last few years is that narratives activate many other parts of our brains as well, suggesting why the experience of reading can feel so alive."

Now, you and I could both likely agree, that the fear level of snakes, from that same book, would swell in that rugged Canadian, weed carpeted reading location. Simply due to the natural environment that it's being read from. It's the exact same words printed on the tree born pages of that book, with exactly the same *you* studying it. What has changed? This has.

The environment. And with it, your state of mind. There is less contradictory info streaming into your brain. Less outside interference. Instead of sitting in your family room, you're now feeling like a guest in the snakes family room. It's like a scary story around a campfire is much scarier than when told in a brightly lit up family room. Isn't it?

Ever had a radio tuned in between stations? Get's all fuzzy. Can't clearly hear either station you're tuner is locked between. Sharpening the sound, is a simple case of pointing the tuner to one station only. Then you can get rockin'. Would it be terrible to think of the readers brain as a tuner? Just for this narration? The message in the snake book is one station, and the outside world is the other. So by altering the environment it reduced contradictory factors. Removed the fuzzy static. The words in the books story, this time, are not being contradicted by the environment around you. Giving the words freedom to stimulate your brain, unencumbered. The words this time, could impart a greater measure of reality. Great emotion.

So with that analogy now laid out accessible in your mind. It's easier to accept that our brain really doesn't make much distinction, between the printed word and the real thing. They both instill emotion generated from the *same* brain regions. The main difference in the two, might be the opposing information which may also be signaling our brain, at the same time we're reading. Causing interference. Keeping the words power subdued. So how could we improve the reality of our words to the reader? Is there a way? How could we change the reading environment?

There is a way. Possibly. **Control the readers *focus.*** In our messages, we have the opportunity to create a conducive setting for our message - *with* our message. We could name this the *"textual environment"*. By controlling the readers focus, with sensory targeted copy, we can reduce the outside world distractions. If the readers brain is fully engaged, they have little left to think about the outside world with. Little left to get distracted by.

The more we keep our readers senses occupied in advance with our words, the less engaged they're able to be with the outside-the-copy world. If their attention is already gripped, by a firm tugging impression of words, their thoughts will be less likely to drift toward other distractions. If their brain is taking heavy fire from multi-sensory neural targeted copy, it could narrow the readers awareness of other things. The readers brain has the power to do this. It's the brains natural way to help us focus on incoming thoughts.

Nine and 1/2

Focus

Focus is treated by some as a life changing power.

My first exposure to Tony Robbins, was reading his teachings on focus. He's taught millions of fans how to transform their lives. By teaching them to control their focus, the world they see looks different.

It changes how we experience life, because the world looks different to us. In reality it's the same world either way. It just looks different and feels different when our focus changes. It can do so, in an instant. Tony uses a focus principle, to transform lives. They love him for it, because it worked. If it works so well for Tony, it could work in our writing too. Right?

Controlling the readers focus, determines the reality they are seeing. And the reality they are **not** seeing.

The method our brain uses to to help us focus, is to block out unrelated information. Sort of like when your wife or husband is talking, but you didn't hear a word they said... Because our focus is on something we considered more important. (Shame on us...:)

In this case those unrelated distractions would be the readers physical environment. But, showering their senses with smell, color, shape, sound, texture and emotion in our message, **transports them out of their physical environment**. Into our textual environment. As I have, I'm sure you've also read a book or watched a movie that just sucked you right in. Just how real can can these word realities get?

Take-Away: *Control their focus* by creating a compelling textual environment. One that keeps the readers senses fully captivated. Triggering multiple sensory targets, fades the outside world. Magnetizing their focus on our message. Influencing their focus, improves how our primary message touches them. The *"textual world"* we create within their mind, sets the believe-ability stage, for our primary message. The same message in a distracting environment, could strike their eyes as less believable.

An angry grizzly, is this really true?

That ole grizzly is going to have to sit tight, just for a moment of space time. Let me share something I just pulled out the air. Over 100 years ago, the primary form of communication, other than face to face, was text. Writing. There were no movies, no youtube, no reality shows. Not even telephone. Ever read a sample of the inked lines, written back in the 1800s or earlier? The now yellowed and cracked paper still hold's their thoughts for us to know. Maybe those sheets are time stained, but no less moving for it. Like the civil war letters. They transport you, along with your heart. Somehow.

"Dear Father, Having a little spare time, I improve it by writing to you.." Can you imagine checking your iphone messages and your eyes finding a text with that style of writing? If you could hold the soldiers script in your hand, even the individual letters in the words themselves were artfully patterned. Their words dressed to embody a proud representation of themselves. Why did they craft lines in such a caring and deliberate way?

Well, maybe it was the only method that could convey, a realistic world which would express the feel and presence of their moment. To lift their experience from one place and send it to someone who wasn't there. Doing it all with words. So they learned to use skillful prose. It's been used for thousands of years for that purpose. Because it worked very well. Until now I fear.

Our generation, hasn't had to rely on the written word, as they have for centuries. We can send a thousand text messages by the time it took ONE letter to be delivered by pony express or the train. They had to make it count. Words were important. Today, it's a new paradigm. Words are cheap, and fast. But not necessarily better. For writers and even marketers today, that changes things. **Words, are the vehicle we use to sell.** In that sense we're a weak generation. Working out our copy muscles, hasn't been as necessary. Since we can more quickly or *"impressively"* communicate by text, video, telephone and TV.

I believe that shift provides a mammoth opening, for writers of this day. The point would be this. It can still be done. We can write in a compelling way that instills reality itself, and moves people. As they've done for centuries before us. Not the outdated language of old, but the artful care and precision of old. The value of word, restored to it's rightful throne and fitted for this new era.

We're standing on ground not yet visited by any before us. With neuroscience enabling our message, we can potentially build a writing skill unlike any time, anywhere. You can do that.

Now, where did that grizzly go? (That's not a question I ever want to find myself asking for real;-)

The angry grizzly. So am I telling you that if you watch an angry grizzly bear on TV, or see the word *"grizzly"* on paper, that you'll get as scared as if you see one in person, in the wild?

You tell me.. Think on this briefly. What if you were watching *yourself* on TV, and the *you* on TV was seeing a grizzly bear in person, in the wild? I'd get a little freaked out I think. Or, what if you were reading a story about *you*, that somebody else wrote. The *you* in the story, was seeing a grizzly bear in person, in the wild! I'd get a little weird with that one too I think.

So I would say, for myself; this word stuff works, but real life still works better. I think that's fair. You have to consider that our brain is not just receiving messages from what we're reading. But also from our surroundings. Aside from that though, science demands that these principles are true. How effective they are, I think would depend on how well our copy is tied together. How expertly we built the story. How well we mingled all of the words and targeted all of the senses.

Multidimensional experiences in copy, are hard to ignore. Hard to deny. Read some of George Orwell's works, like his *Shooting the Elephant* story. There is no escape from his lines. On the following day after I read it, I was still re-reading it again in my mind. The thoughts and words stuck with me. They went in deep, because he writes so well. That's what great writing can do.

Flat one dimensional writing could be easy for our brains to dismiss. Why? Maybe because much of the brain is not being called to use. Reality has many dimensions, not just one. Then shouldn't our content?

Chucking words to only a limited number of brain zones or senses, leaves most of their brain team on the bench. Those benched brain players, aren't built to do nothing.

Who likes to sit on the bench? Not my brain. I want get in the game, make a great play, or even score a touch down. If we don't send the reader's neurons into the game, or hit the ball to them, they'll find another game that does.

Nine and 3/4

Words versus Movies.

Some novelists can make a book more real than a great movie. That's what I've heard a few readers say, and I'd agree. Many movies are said to disappoint people who have read the books, prior to seeing the movie on screen.

Even so, great movies have made people jump out of their seats in fear. And afterwards stay up at night and carry fears with them, their entire lives. If great copy can be as gripping than movies, then I'd say both can be very real.

Neuroscience Research Lab at Berkeley is where Brian Pasley does research. Dark hair covers his head, and he looked younger than I expected. One night he stated on a TV broadcast, that internalized thoughts, activate the same places in the brain that audible language does.

Sometimes internalized thought can even be heard [by the person thinking it] according to Brian. So let's apply that principle to our prospect or readers. As a reader thinks about what they are reading, internalizing the text, they are activating the same spots in their brain as if they were having an audible conversation. So their brain is reacting as if the words were spoken with sound. But there is one difference.

The sound their brains are hearing in a typed message is the sound they personalize to those words. Their imagination plays a roll in creating the sound they read. So each reader may hear a somewhat different sound. As opposed to speaking the words in person, all would hear the same sound of the speaker.

If I asked you to recall a recent dream, which one would it be? If you would, please pull your favorite dream experience up, in your mind. Stop reading for a few seconds and just think about it.

In that dream, how real did that world seem at the time you were having it- while you were sleeping? The YOU in your dream I'll wager, was very convinced that the world your own mind created (the dream world) ,was extremely real. 100% percent real.

Couldn't get any more real. People (including me) have woken up sweating or scared to death from some dreams. Thanking God we wake up, because in the dream sometimes it looks like were done for. And we believe it. Some people talk up a level five storm in their sleep. The person laying next to them can actually hear the sleepers sentences. So they obviously believe it's real. That doesn't happen unless our thoughts, in the dream, are truly perceived as reality.

So our dreams are very real - until we wake up. Sometimes though, even after we wake up, at least for a handful of minutes - *we can still see the dream imagery clearly.* Still feel the emotion. Dreams can even inspire us on occasion. Inspire us, in the "awake" world. Something interesting is proven by that dream experience.

That our brain has the full capability within itself, to generate what we truly believe is reality. In this light, couldn't it be argued that reality comes from our brain, and not from the outside world?

In fact, science cannot even prove that what we choose believe is reality, is in fact real. It's just what we perceive is real. Perception is reality.

So, if our brains have the power to generate a complete reality in our dreams. Out of empty air, using nothing but our own mind activity - then we know something else too.

The readers brain is capable of making great copy completely believable to the reader. The only question is, how real can we make our copy to their brain?

The brain can generate a reality, if we can write it.

This is the whole point of *this book*. How to make our copy, real to the brain. Here's a head scratcher. It's the position taken by some novelist, that words can actually deliver what reality cannot deliver. Word has the power to go beyond visual simulation such as TV and even to go beyond reality itself. How can this be?

Words allow the reader to see words through the movie screen of their own experiences. That is the subject of upcoming Chapter Nineteen. You'll come up on it, before we hit the *story* section.

Sensory rich words give our copy a physical dynamic. It does this by activating the same regions of the brain that physical reality activates. A true-to-life life dynamic, spawned by text. This idea was taken even one step further...

Emory University researcher Krish Sathian has shown how words can impact our emotional experience of a sentence as we read. Just by changing <u>one word</u>. In this test two different phrases were compared:

"Having a bad day?" versus *"Having a rough day?"*

Note the word *"rough"* replaced the word *"bad"*. Rough is a touch sensory word. Like *"sandpaper"* which also delivers abrasive connotations.

It turns out the second phrase which used the word *"rough"*, triggered the sensory part of the brain that deals with physical touch. The first phrase did not activate that part of the brain.

That's heavy fact. Inserting touch based sensory words (used as adjectives), targets and then stimulates a readers touch senses. *"Leathery hands"* would trigger a touch sensory area, where *"strong hands"* would not. The brain treated the textured words, as a physical reality. **Shabaam!**

With motion words, the brain sends the words outside the language processing area to the motor cortex. It's sort of on the top of your brain according to the picture I looked up. The motor cortex, according to Wikipedia, is the part of the brain that plans and controls voluntary movement. Like throwing, kicking running, jumping etc. This is worth repeating, because this puzzle piece is a perfect fit.

Motion *words,* are also sent out of the language processing area, to the same part of the brain that controls *physical* motion.

Even breaking the destination down to sub-sections of the motor cortex, depending on whether the motion of a body part was an arm or a leg. That made me wonder something else.

Whether muscle activation could authentically be triggered by words. You know, like the finger tip sitting on top of a mouse button. Does the brain stop short at activating muscles, if prompted by words? In Chapter Twelve we'll explore that question.

A distinct, perceptible experience for the brain, is created through targeted sensory wordage. Could this *word play* actually increase sales? Or does the theory fall apart when real money is on the line?

Well, let's just pay a visit to Cornell University and find out, shall we? If you can't trust Cornell, who can you trust?

In fact over at good ole Cornell University, Brian Wansink and two of his fellow researchers, control tested that very thing. Now Brian is somewhat of food and marketing super hero.

You may recall in recent history when food menus started to be more healthful. Brian was behind some of that. He's won dozens of awards. His nickname is "The Wizard of Why". Even had a White House appointment with the USDA. Authored more complicated articles than we could read in a month. And let's not forget authoring multiple books.

It's safe to say the world is healthier because of Brian. His areas of expertise include Behavioral Economics and Consumer Behavior to pick just 2 of the 9. The look on his face in the pic, suggested to me he's still holding back much of what he knows. With such devoted experience, you'd expect his blonde well groomed hair, to show a bit more shock and tangle, along the lines of Albert Einstein's.

Using emotional and sensory word triggers. i.e. Plump, juicy, freshly squeezed,"Succulent Italian Seafood Filet" etc. the testing began. They structured this research with a split test methodology, such as "Grilled Chicken" versus "Tender Grilled Chicken". How about "Snappy Carrots"? Sounds good to me. Barely a day goes by when I don't chomp one down. Results were collected week after week, for 6 weeks.

The descriptive **adjectives used on food menus increased food sales by27%**.

They didn't change the price, or the menu colors, just a few of the words to target specific brain regions.

They scientifically increased sales by targeting those brain regions with sensory rich words. Thanks Brian, I won't soon forget that fact... ..but now I'm hungry..:).

In fact, it did more than just increase sales. It also improved the customers attitudes about the experience, to the point of **being more willing to return**. "Repatronage" they called it. Something else was typed into the report.

That the surveyed customers **would be willing to pay 10% more for each descriptive item**. But there seems to be a catch.

Brakes on. Put it in park. Turn off the key...We need to talk.

There is one critical detail we *must* remember, when deploying descriptive copy.. And it's the ONLY way it will work. (P.S. you've just been brain hacked - I'll explain later:).

Descriptive copy must be.....(tight drum roll please.)........wait for it...........

.......the magic word is : **DETCEPSXENU!** Ooops...I spelled it backwards.. **It's Unexpected!** Dude, I'm trying to keep your right brain from getting board... I mean bored. Righty wants to have fun too ya know.. Okay, let's get all serious again and see how to make some MONEY, by brain-hackng da' people!!!

Ten

"Surprise, surprise, surprise."

<u>Unexpected</u> words are the key, to making it work. Okay, freeze! Right where you are. If you would, take that word "Unexpected" and blow it up in your mind. Bigger. NO, real big. As big as your car. Now paint it red, bright red. Because that is the most important word in this entire book. If you only remember one word from this book, remember UNEXPECTED. It's the single most important key to unlocking the brain of your prospect or reader. Here's why.

Our brain forces familiar information into our subconscious. Without processing it like it would unfamiliar information. The reason is so we can use our focus on the unfamiliar and unexpected.

Great copy must engage the readers focus. We need the readers fore-brain in the game. Because it activates more neurons, as it analyzes the unexpected words and phrases. More neurons equals more engagement. We want the reader to think about what we say. Even feel it. We can't sell to a reader that's sleep-reading.

Example. Saying "Thank you" means almost nothing. Because we've all heard it so much. It just bounces off the brain. Saying "Hey, Thanks" or "Double thanks!" would feel much more sincere as it is read. More feeling means a more responsive reader.

The reason it would feel more sincere is because the reader's brain would actually be sending the unexpected phrase to more places. As it analyzes the phrase. Literally a deeper thought is formed. Creating with it, more feeling. So if you really want someone to know you're grateful. It must be written in an uncommon way. It's the only way your "thank you" will actually be delivered to the emotional centers of the brain.

Every thought carries with it an emotional biochemical. In essence every thought is an electro-chemical. These chemicals are needed for storage of the memory, and create physical reactions as well.

Thoughts, images,sounds, textures all change into electro-chemical format. *"All information in the brain is in electo-chemical format."* (Leaf 2009, p. 29).

So the depth of thought we generate in our reader, partly determines what they feel.

Of course certain types and intensity of thoughts create certain types and intensity of chemicals. The fewer and shallower thoughts that we have, the less we feel. For example, these two phrases were tested at Emory University in 2012; "The singer had a velvety voice" versus "The singer had a pleasing voice". Fewer brain regions were activated in the second phrase. (Paul 2012)

The surprise factor plays a key role in reader brain reaction. For creating neural tuned copy, this is a primary factor to consider. This was concluded in a very recent study. *"..revealing a strong relation between the surprisal of a word and the amplitude of the N400* [The EEG measurement] *component in response to reading that word."* (Frank,2015).

Overly familiar words excite fewer neurons, so they would lose their stimulating qualities. Like seeing a movie for the first time as opposed to the second, third or fourth time. The surprise factor would be zapped. So expected words suck. Unexpected words rock.

Played out words or phrases, will drop dead in a readers mind. fMRI imaging has shown, through a study that our brains stop overused words dead in their tracks. Like shooting blanks instead of lead bullets. Writing with stale, played out words and phrases is no more effective than shooting a slobbering, full galloped grizzly bear in the brain, with a *blank*.

They have small effect on the human brain. (And the grizzly.) Other than boredom. An unexpected word or phrase is like shooting a lead bullet. A neural-tuned phrase is like shooting a silver bullet.

Common phrases like *"Have a nice day"*, *"hotter than hell"* , *"I could eat a horse"* etc. will likely not activate neurons as much as **unfamiliar** or **unexpected** phrases with the same meaning. Catch that one, it's gold.

It's a major league point, that will play a pivotal role in all of your copy, sales, conversions and clicks. For the rest of our typing life.

That principle can change a readers mind. **Fresh copy activates more neurons. More neurons means more emotion.**

Over played language, phrases, words and metaphors, doesn't show the increased neural activity. Keep it fresh. Original.

Imagine if you bought a ticket for a comedy stand-up act. Once the comedian began his routine, you realized something. That his jokes were the same jokes you heard last week, at another stand up routine. In fact they were the same jokes you heard two months prior, and at every other stand up act. This comedian was re-joking. How far could that comedians career take him? **ShaBamm!**

How is our writing any different? Whether we're writing a book, email, ad, blog or writing a joke.

Readers, like a comedian's audience, want to be surprised. The reader is the happiest when they are being surprised by the content. Engaging the reader *literally* requires neuron activity. Keep it fresh, original. (Did you notice that's the same phrase as 3 paragraphs above? :-)

If we don't, our message may quickly sink into the abyss. That would be a Titanic copy mistake. Though many times we have to use common words. There is a way to use them and still be effective.

Example City... Step out, walk around and take the tour. Welcome to "Example City"

If we have to use common words, then rearrange them to create a new meaning. Or use them in a new context. Like Nike did. Yep, Nike brain hacked da' people! They took three common words, *"Just do it"* , which used to mean stuff like *"clean your room"* or *"eat your greens"* or *"take your medicine"*. Mom or Dad would say *"just do it"*. Before Nike got a hold of it, the phrase was usually meant to do something you didn't want to do, like chores. Nike used the must-do phrase, in a whole new context. The context of sports achievement! The context of greatness.

Which rocks! Who doesn't like greatness? Totally unexpected, and universally cool. **By using the phrase in a new context, they changed the meaning of the phrase.** In doing that, Nike gave three common words, a stunning board-walk make over.

With a motivating new meaning. Now it says, *"Just be totally awesome and break all the limits."* , *"Win the game"*. It means *"Just be great"*. It means *"I am great if I'm wearing Nike stuff, because I just freakin' do it!"*. Note how that last line shows how the customer identifies them-self with the Nike brand attitude. (More persuasions from Nike are coming up in Chapter Eighteen.)

Here's another example: Standing in a shivering walk-in freezer you can say "Its hotter than hell in here.", and it might just activate the listeners funny bone brain region. However, if we say the same phrase "It's hotter than hell in here." while standing in a hot green house, you will only get a yawn from the listener. It has no real emotional value in an overused context. The phrase has two different meanings depending on where and how you use it. So...

It's okay to use a common phrase, if done in an uncommon way. Same with a common word. Same with multiple assembled common words. If we say "hows the weather out side?" while standing in our *living room*, we'll hear crickets. It's just a boring question. But, if we say it while standing in the *International Space Station* when it's 200 below zero outside, it has a different meaning. We won't bore the other astronauts, they might even laugh. Same sentence, different context.

Be creative in word and phrase choice, to activate more brain real estate. See I just did it. Combining <u>brain</u> and <u>real estate,</u> It's an unexpected combination. It makes your brain stop and think about it. **Fresh words and phrases are a readers drug.** It's a wake up pill. I just gave you a drug. Really. Because it created a chemical in your brain when you read it, and you liked it :-)

Just remember, old words and phrases are like old jokes. Or old news. The first time you hear a joke, is it funny? The first time you see news it's interesting. It should be, right? The second time you hear it, your brain is not quite as impressed is it? Not like it was the first time.

It's the same principle working in a readers brain. Fresh content stimulates more neurons. If you notice in this book, I tried to not be entirely predictable. That's why some phrases I wrote are worded differently that one might expect. As you keep reading you'll find more like that. It was deliberate.

At the risk of sounding politically incorrect - **Don't recycle**. Words and phrases that is. **See if you can catch another example in the next line.**

Take-Away: *"Just say No"* - to *stale* words or phrases. Keep it *fresh* and *unexpected.* Keep em' guessing. Choose words that they don't see coming. Rephrase and refresh. Overplayed language bores the readers brains. Especially righty.

Let's see which words work the best.

Eleven

Negatives... do they sell?

Ever wonder whether you should be positive in your copy as opposed to negative?

This chapter is a key building block, in the copywriting foundation. We know, according to what we just read in Chapter Nine, descriptive words can increase sales. They improve customer loyalty. They can raise our products perceived value.

Since it was university proven, we could honestly say, it's a scientifically proven fact. Each one of these writing parameters, like the one were about to explore, has monetary value, if used in marketing copy.

But more than that, they offer us guidelines to better tune in to the reception of a readers brain. Locking our message on to the same frequency that our brain is naturally designed to operate in. Each one, adds another building block to your foundation. But greater than that, we're enabled to truly reach people. Elevating the reading *experience*.

More fully engaging their mind. We're building this foundation, scientifically. As opposed to just marketing split tests results. Split testing tells us IF something worked. It doesn't tell us WHY it worked. Neural tuned copy, is based on knowing WHY our copy should work. So let's look at Negative vs. Positive words and see why one may or may not be better than the other.

Could Negative words slammed the brakes on thought?

Bangor University did a blind study reported by NBC News (LiveScience 2012). A group of Chinese participants who were English speaking, agreed to have their brains scanned when participating in a reading study. They were told to compare meanings of paired English words. Remember this crucial fact- **these readers were Chinese but also spoke English as their *second* language.**

The test words were all in English --their second language. Then they were to press a button if the two word meanings were similar. So they were shown multiple pairs of words, one pair at a time. Each time, they were instructed to compare the two words to see if they were similar in meaning. All of the words were in their second language, English. But there was a secret twist. There was a detail the researchers didn't tell them.

Little did the participants know, the actual study was focused on an entirely different agenda. Yep, they were tricked. What was actually being measured, **was their brains reaction to *positive* versus *negative* words.**

The pairs of words they were being shown were either positive or negative. You see, the researchers were tracking which language section of the brain (primary or secondary) the words were sent to. There's a very good reason the researchers did it.

Here's why this was important; our primary language is where the bulk of our thought and definitions come from. When reading in a second language we have to access our primary language also, in order to process that thought in our native tongue. **We get the definition of words from our native tongue.** Turns out, the readers being tricked weren't the only one's in for a surprise.

What the researchers found, was the **exact** **opposite** of what they expected. *"Extremely surprised"*, was how researchers Wu and Guillaume Thierry phrased it. (2012)

They discovered that **our brains refuse to think about negative words**. Refuse.

Is it logical to say our brain has a mind of it's own? Apparently in this case it could be logical. It was a subconscious behavior--they couldn't help it.) The MRI scanners could detect when the readers were accessing their native language versus the English language regions of their brain.

When the readers encountered negative words, **they did not even access the native speaking region** of their brain. Positive words had a different effect. Those words engaged both English and Native language regions. A neuro-roadblock, was halting negative words from being fully processed. Their brains were automatically shutting down the negative thoughts. Imagine that..

Negative words prompted an internal reaction. **They triggered a protective mechanism.**

Possibly to safeguard us from negative or damaging emotions. Remember, every thought carries with it, a corresponding chemical. So negative thoughts would produce harmful chemicals and hormones. Canceling the thought process of the negative words, would reduce harmful chemical production.

Their brains withheld negative information from their conscious thoughts. May 8th 2012, An article describing this was published in Livescience. It was titled "Brain ...represses bad words...".

Writing copy without this knowledge, would be like trying to shoot a Star Trek laser beam though a force field. It wouldn't get through.

Like trying to hit a target with our eyes closed. Our words would miss their mark. They're reach into the brain is reduced. Almost like a muting effect. Like knocking on the door when nobody is home. Negative words don't get let in.

Optimized neural tuned copy avoids those type of wasteful misfires, and locks in on high value targets.

It's why I said earlier, that it's more possible these days, to know in advance how our words will react in our readers brain--if we're aware of some of these neural sensory targeting concepts.

Knowing WHY we write what we write, is what this style of copywriting is all about. Allowing us the opportunity to tactically construct a compelling message that stands a greater chance to be received. One we know their brain will welcome.

Past versus Present

Travel back in time, to 1923, United States of America. A historical marketing book was published. This particular book is often at the absolute top of the list, when citing works that revolutionized marketing. In his book "Scientific Advertising", Claude Hopkins also promoted a marketing principle regarding negative versus positive copy.

The very comparison we just covered in this chapter. Only we looked at it from a technological science lab standpoint. Would those findings confirm or deny Claude's principle? How would Claude's 1923 writing principle stand up to these fMRI findings, 91 years later?

Surprisingly, Claude's immovable position on these lines, were almost identical to these recent scientific results. Claude suggested to always bring out the positive, never the negative. *"...always appear a good fellow."*(Hopkins, 1923, C. 18). Even if it's about the competition.

Little did he plan 91 years later, to have an fMRI verify his conclusion. It has been suggested, that positive versus negative advertising copy out-converts to the tune of four to one. Claude proved it worked. Now we know *why* it worked.

Take-away: To get deeper brain connection, *keep it positive*. Negative words turn the lights off, in our readers brain. To bypass the brains protective shielding and promote conversion, promote the positive only.

Twelve

Can the power of written words, trigger muscle action?

Emotional Verbs and physical response.

August 10, Amsterdam Netherlands. A group of students there, were wired and given a series of words to read. Specifically emotional verbs. For example *"to smile"*, *"to cry"*. In contrast they were given non-verb words with similar meanings. For example *"funny"* and *"frustrating"*.

While reading, the students were being monitored for facial muscle activation. What researcher, Francesco, found was that the exact same muscles, we use for smiling, were activated when reading "to smile"

At the same time, The muscles used for frowning were not activated when reading *"to smile"*. These emotional verbs, caused more muscle activation than even adjectives of the same meaning. For example: *"to laugh"* caused more activation than "funny". *"To cry"* caused more muscle activation than *"frustrating"*.

The researchers concluded that muscle activity was induced in the reader, when reading emotional *verbs*, representing facial expressions of emotion. I call these action verbs. This study was published in the journal of Psychological Science. (cited aps, n.d.).

What happens when we apply action verbs to a button? One marketing company did a split test of two phrases. One you may have used, yourself in the past. It's a very common offer. They compared "Free Trial" with a similar phrase using verbs. "Try it for free". What they found was a 20% increase in conversion using the second verb laced phrase. Action can be induced in our reader to some degree, by using action verbs.

Is it possible to motivate a reader to click their mouse button using related action verbs in the copy? That answer will have to remain a mystery for now.

Take-Away: Emotional verbs give one of the strongest pushes. They lead to physical action. Conversion can be increased by introducing verbs into our call to action. Add an emotional sensory dimension to your message and trigger physical muscle reactions.

Letting the reader feel the action, and take action.

Thirteen

How to set the hook at the end of paragraph.

Like the karate kid Swan-Technique - *"When done properly --no can defense."* (Karate Kid -Kesuke Miyagi).

Ever wonder why we hate commercials? I did. It's because of the set up. We are baited with suspense, right before commercial break. That way we're sure to stay tuned. It works. But lately, it's getting so blatant, you can see the commercial coming like a jet liner rolling down a roadway. They telegraph it. Every climactic moment these days, is just a set up for a commercial.

A commercial is nearly always preceded by a perceived climactic moment. And a good chunk of the time, the climatic moment winds up being an edited contrivance. Made to look like suspense just hook us for the commercial break. Of course they don't show us that letdown, until after the commercial.

What we can learn from that is this: We know they need a hook, or we're going bye bye at the commercial break. Ever pull in a fish without a hook? They'll forfeit viewers without the hook. It is an essential part of TV programming and marketing.

Should it be any less important for copywriters?

From the days when your ancient ancestors walked sandal footed across the land, we've communicate using stories. Our brains have habitually evolved to try and piece things together in story form. We can't help it. In fact even as kids we loved it. How many times have your young kids responded to your statement with "*Why*"?

We can't stand to have an uncompleted story. That's why we hate commercials. We hate commercials because we're left hanging. Our story was not concluded, and we have to have it finished. So we stick around for the conclusion of the climactic moment.

Best selling author and story expert Nick Nanton detailed this "story effect" principle, in his book *Story Telling*. Nick literally creates celebrity status in his clients, by using this story principle. The principle of people loving stories.

Ever heard a rumor you *weren't* eager to listen to? Can a rumor be stopped? Answer: No, they don't stop, they grow until they're plump and juicy as a sweet summer peach. Yum! Like a peach, they grow naturally. Because people love to listen to, learn about and tell stories.

We think in story form. It's how our brains work best. Whether we're two or ninety two. The only reason we like facts, is because we use them to create and prove our stories. Research has proven this. So, how can our love of stories improve our marketing, today? How can it improve our writing?

Word Glue

(How to keep a reader Glued to our message.)

Here's a few concepts that apply to authors as well as marketing copywriters. It's a question every marketer and blogger wants to know. How can we keep a reader *glued* to our writing?

By hooking them. Literally. Hooking them with a ? A question mark looks like a hook don't it? :-)

End your paragraph with a question. Like I just did. Yes, you were just baited with a question:-) I told you it works. Don't use just any random question. But a question that will be answered in the next paragraph or two. An Open question. "Open" means the answer could go any number of ways. In other words the answer is unknown, when you ask it. It holds attention like reader glue.

The Open Question

An Open question at the end of a paragraph, is leading the reader to where we intend on taking them next. It's opening the door for them. Asking them to follow you through that door. A door that leads to the next paragraph.

Think of your end-of-paragraph question as the hook, that keeps them on the line. Open questions create curiosity, and suspense. It also floats a subconscious idea. An idea of mystery in our story, which is drama. It's a little mystery, which is about to be solved. But only in the next paragraph. Who's going to turn and walk away from a story, right before the mystery gets solved? Not me.

Curiosity is an emotion. It has emotional pull. It's also a clever persuasion tool. It breaks the less appealing pattern of me *telling* you what I think. That's unappealing because what it's actually doing is directing you to what you should think. I don't like to be told what to think, and if you're like me, you don't either. Neither does our prospect. By asking instead of telling --a subconscious positive transformation of how our reader perceives us, begins to occur. Yep.

This new positive pattern, is the notion that the evidence will speak for itself. When the question is answered. The evidence will do the telling. To both of us. My position then is seen by the reader in a more objective light. Authoritative statements can be threatening, intimidating or even arrogant. Questions are a friendlier way to outlay our point. Especially *open* questions.

Open questions such as *"what did you do yesterday"* allows a broad participatory response. It's conversational. A basic yes or no question would limit the amount of participation the reader could inject. Pulling the reader into the conversation, keeps them engaged, and therefore reading. Especially critical at the closing of a paragraph. It's a high value Golden Gate bridge, leading over the treacherous water where we could lose them if we're not careful. The bridge leads them to the next paragraph.

A question **glues** the paragraphs breaks together. Getting stuck in the word glue, is the reader. Not wanting to leave the answer behind, the reader moves to the next paragraph. In pursuit of the reveal. In pursuit of a cliff hanger answer to their story. The one we're always trying to weave in their mind.

Paragraphs are essential, to break up the copy. Long paragraphs suck. They're are as bad as long sentences. Both spook readers. The trick, is to not lose the reader on the break. Using an open question helps adhere the reader to the message, through the breaks.

Take-Away: Mentally chain the reader to your copy by ending the paragraph with a question. *Open* questions leave a wide opening for a variety of answers. Rather than a Yes or No answer, which limits their participation.

Fourteen

Armor Piercing persuasion tool.

(How to use a *Loaded Leading Question*. I've even used this one on my mom.. sorry mom :(

Let's try a quickie writers test.

Read the first italicized statement below, then read the second. Which is more persuasive in getting the reader to acknowledge and believe my point? The subject is: Writing as if to a single person rather than a group of people.

Version 1: *Writing our copy as if to one person, will work better than writing as if to a group.*

Version 2: *Would you rather be written to as a individual, or be written to impersonally, as part of a group?*

Do you see what just happened? In the First version , I TOLD the reader what works. As if I'm the boss, and know more than them. As if I am teacher and they are student. Sort of an arrogant delivery.

In the second version I found a kinder, suggestive way to let the reader teach themselves. A more convincing way. Let's score the two and see who wins.

The Second version hit 4 targets.

1. I asked the <u>reader's</u> opinion. Which shows I value their opinion.

2. I got the reader to <u>participate</u>. Now we're *sharing* the experience together. Having a conversation, where both of us are talking. We're in agreement.

3. I've also let the reader <u>tell themselves</u> the answer. (People trust themselves more than anyone). I simply reminded them of a belief which they already had.

4. I <u>engaged</u> more parts of the readers brain, by getting them and their imagination involved in a response. Sparking deeper thought, enhanced their experience. Adding greater depth and more dimension to my copy.

The First version not only missed all 4 targets, it caused collateral damage in three ways.

1. I bored the reader, by not engaging them.

2. I offended the reader by sounding arrogant.

3. It was less effective in driving home my point.

The answer to version two's question was obvious. So it was an easy lay up. I knew in advance what their answer would be. I just wanted them to come to their own conclusion. Both versions are intended to convey the same message. Which version do you feel was more effective? If you said two, slap me five! Cha ching baby, we got this.

Which style of copy do you more commonly come across in marketing content? Exactly, number one. Another fiver dude!

End of test.

Take-Away: Use *Loaded Leading* questions to prompt the reader to <u>recall</u> what they already believe, from past experiences. An armor piercing *recall* persuasion tool.

The Invisible *Phantom* question.

(How to stealth-fully get the reader to ask you a question.)

Remember in Chapter Nine when I said *"P.S. You've just been brain hacked...I'll explain later."* ? Well, guess what time it is? It's later.

I used the *Phantom* type question we're about to cover. In that Chapter Nine brain hack, I got you to ask me a question (internally), and got you to want to keep reading to find the answer. It too is powerful near the end of a paragraph. That's exactly when I used it also.

This is a covert asset. Authentically. It pops a question right into a readers mind. A question that they will quietly ask us to answer. An answer, which they will keep reading to find.

It's simple. **Just inject curiosity.** Do it like this: *"Opening my mail yesterday I had a nice little surprise"*. That's it. Seriously, that's it. Doesn't look like much does it? Simple right? The curiosity seed has been planted though. They will not leave until they get the answer of what I found in my mail. Of course, we try plant the seed in to our preceding story lines. Just lay it out there, and they'll pick it up. Here's how it works.

After reading an inconclusive statement, the reader instantly internalizes a question. Directed at us. The question is *"What was the surprise in the mail that you found?"* By stating (or baiting) the clue, we've literally **dropped a question into their mind. A question they now *want* you to answer.**

I love that tiny trick. Because once I lay the trap, I know they want to know what I have to tell them. A slightly "I'm important to you now" feeling comes over me. (For a brief moment:-)

Do it near the end of a paragraph and they'll leap with you, right over to the next paragraph. Like stepping stones across a river. The *phantom* question was our second type of leading question. Before we get to the third, please make note of these 3 types. Open, Loaded Leading and Phantom.

I'll explain that in a moment. First lets look at the third and final piece to the "leading question" puzzle. The third and final piece of the question puzzle is the **Compound question.** Sometimes referred to as a *double barreled* question.

Take-Away: Use a *Phantom* question to get the reader to ask you a question. It's an answer they will be eager to pursue. Do this, by introducing curiosity. Make an inconclusive statement, and leave them hanging. Just until the next paragraph or two. Example: *"The results were something I never expected".*

Fifteen

The double-barreled question. (Just as bad-ass it sounds)

How to cut the life blood out of sales pressure. (And persuade the reader at the very same time!)

To instill **Trust** in addition to **suspense** and **curiosity,** use a <u>compound leading question</u>. A double question. Such as this spin: *Would an A/B split test confirm this theory? Or would the theory fall flat on it's tender face if put to that test?*

Now in the compound question above, there's two parts. I subtlety introduced even more objectivity, than with a single line question. This question puts a fork in the road.

A choice for the reader to consider internally, and make on their own. Notice the complete absence of pressure to convince them? Absence of overt pressure. Instead, it harnesses the power of **covert** persuasion. Suggesting the notion that a split test could possibly prove my theory **false.**

That the result could either be false or true. Like it's out of my hands. It demonstrates, I am not hiding anything. Not trying to convince them of anything. It says, *we are going by the evidence. Not by my opinion.* In doing that, I've persuaded them that I'm not trying to sell them. Which should grow trust. Both in me as well as the evidence I am presenting.

Letting the reader come to their own conclusion. It postions me as an **unbiased observer**. Just like them. I'm seen more as a **narrator** than a pushy salesman. A presenter of facts. **Creating trust.** Following the compound question, they would be eager to see the undisclosed results. Which I actually knew in advance that I would show them, while setting up the compound question. The reader would internalize an answer to the question. Involuntarily participating in the conversation with me.

Take Away: Use *Compound* questions to introduce a challenge, or possibility of doubt for your product or message. It creates drama. Like a bladed Ninja, it will slip in and **slice** the sales pressure cord cleanly. That cord could have pulled the reader away from us. Best of all our upcoming answer will make the product or message look victorious. That victory occurs when we answer the question positively in the next paragraph or two.

Sixteen

Steroids for Copy

(The smallest, most powerful and least used character on your keyboard, is the PERIOD.)

Think of the period as little *steroids for copy*. Little pills, that beef up your results.

It's reported that USA press associations have laid down a readability table. It relates to sentence length. Based on several studies they collected some facts to help the writers. Or I should say, to help the readers. Their survey shows that readers find sentences of 8 words or less very easy to read. The sentence you just read was about 12 words. They found 11 words easy. With 17 words they considered it standard. In the 21-25 word range, they said it's fairly difficult. Encountering 30 words or more was said to suck. Well not exactly suck, that was my paraphrase. They graded it 30+ as very difficult. What's the reason for this?

Martin Cutts, author of Oxford Guide to Plain English, suggested a similar theory. Referring to why people don't like long sentences. He said "People fear and recoil from snake like sentences. Rather than full stops" [periods]. It's why we should *never* put a long sentence at the beginning of a paragraph. Unless we don't want them to read it :) So check out these numbers.

If 17 words are an average sentence length. According to the survey. And those surveyed, preferred only 8 word sentences. That means readers prefer an average of 53% more periods in the messages they read. Short sentences are more appealing to readers. If that's true. And if we're trying to persuade our readers of something, wouldn't it make more sense to use shorter sentences?

Veronica Roth is the author of some finger burning, hot books lately. One is called "Divergent". If you can steal a chance to scan some lines of her books (highly recommended for successful writing style study), you'll notice something. That "something", relates to this chapter.

She kicks many of her paragraphs off with one lil' short sentence. Just a three or four word sentence.

Makes sense too, in my mind. Readers could be more inclined to start reading a paragraph if the first sentence looks quick and easy. Once they take that first bite, it's easier to keep them reading the next line.

Going back to Martin Cutts comment "People fear and recoil from snake like sentences.", a long sentence could scare people away from a paragraph. If that long sentence was the first sentence in the paragraph especially. But why don't readers like long sentences? What happens in a readers brain as they're consuming a sentence?

For a reader to interpret a sentence, they must first accumulate and store all the information within it. It's done using their ***"working"*** short term memory. It's a category of memory which helps us focus on what is directly in front of us. It's limited in capacity for one thing. It can only hold so much. Just like your stomach with food.. Once you're full, you don't want any more. There's also a another characteristic which makes the "working memory" corruptible for long sentences. It has quicker memory decay. So, the readers don't like long sentences because our brain is not designed to handle long sentences. Long sentences require more storage.

The "working memory" doesn't have it. Longer duration of storage also. Longer delay in concluding the thought as well. In the short - more mental work. Longer sentences require more working memory. And sometimes we just don't have it.

Increasing the chance the information will be forgotten or over crowded, before we reach the period. The sentence could fall apart in our mind, before it's ever completed. Our minds have a limited working memory, so doesn't it make sense that readers would "recoil" from long sentences?

What's the point of a sentence? As a reader is gobbling up a sentence, they are asking themselves ONE question the entire time. Every sentence we read causes us to ask this same question. The question is :"What's the point of this sentence?". They are looking for the period, waiting for it, in order to answer this question. When ever there's a pause, or word break, or comma, this question automatically pops to mind. The question is this: What's the point?

They are anticipating the *POINT*. The only reason they start reading a sentence in the first place, is to learn the *point*. When we are required to accumulate a huge pile of words, in order to learn that point, then we'll think twice before starting the next sentence. Repeated procrastinating points, create *micro-stress*. It's less fun to read.

By not having short sentences, we are stressing their brain. Dragging them through the word swamp. Word after word ....after word. With no reward. No point can be awarded until the period is reached. The thought is not concluded, and cannot be concluded, if the period hasn't yet been found. They're not just looking for the period, they're hoping for the period. Why not give it to them?

It's been found in studies that longer sentences induce *"skipping"*. We don't want skippers do we? Human brains can only retain so much information in a short amount of time. Once the tank is full, guess what happens? In one ear and out the other so to "speak". (lil' play on words with words there. Ohhh the thickness of the irony of it all.:-). Obviously nobody would enjoy or comprehend reading, if the message was being pushed directly out the other side. Onto the floor. We have trouble holding any more info before we swallow what we already bit off. We don't want to choke the poor dude with words. Our "working memory" it's said, has a chunk size limit, and a time limit. Like ram on a computer is only for short term stuff. The hard drive on a computer is for longer term storage. Same with our human brain computer. Thirty Seconds they say is about as long as we should speak at a time.

After that, give the listener time to process it. A handy number to store in mind when sizing up paragraph length's too, wouldn't you say? Thirty seconds. Of course there is a perfect time for longer sentences. Strategically tailoring sentence length is apparently important for the reader though. And they're right. For retention and impact purposes, it can pay off. It's hard for any message to be compelling, unless it's absorbed. Shorter sentences are more easily absorbed.

Not that there isn't a place for a longer sentence. In fact there is a special ability which longer sentences carry. An ability a short sentences could never accomplish. The longer sentence structure is saved for Chapter Nineteen. Where I can craft the *tall sword of copy*, in the detail it deserves.

Short sentences are easier to decipher. Create less reader stress. They draw the reader in. Forcing them to interpret every closed statement. So they can move on the the next one. To believe the sentence - or not. Bite size content, is easier to serve. More tempting to mentally partake of.

And then there's always the Catch

The period allows them, to establish belief. Belief equals **trust**. To conclude the thought is to end doubt. Until they reach the period, **belief is suspended**. It must be, because there could be a *catch*. They're waiting for the *catch*, which they believe is certainly coming. And it usually does. Right?

Subconsciously readers expect a catch. Above all with long sentences. Short sentences reverse that in-bent thought pattern. With a short sentence, they must suspend **dis**belief. A period eliminates the possibility of *"the catch"*. It tells them, there was no catch. The sentence is over. It's a finite proposition. The longer the sentence is, the more guarded they become. Short sentences garner more trust. The shorter. The better. Period. SEE? Introducing the **"micro sentence"**..

Takeaway: Use *Short sentences* at the beginning of paragraphs, Always weigh the cost of long sentences. Readers prefer less not more. Split your sentence in two, or shorten it when ever possible. Makes easier absorption. More believable.

Use the *period*, liberally.

Seventeen

The Micro Sentence

Charles Bukowski is one of the worlds more recognized authors (65 books) . Also a contributor to multiple magazines. This pic below is fittingly Charles Bukowski, smoking. (courtesy Wiki-August 2008 Tyrenius). His copy reads as the picture looks. Strong character with unrepentant flaws.

"Genius might be the ability to say a profound thing in a simple way." -- Charles Bukowski.

A crude man with an unpolished tongue. Or so he would make it appear. Down to earth, unapologetic and almost lethal writing. Short dry sentences. They're his hallmark. He made them famous. Many are just 4 or 5 words long. Grab one of his books. Most book stores carry several. "*Post Office*" is my suggestion. You'll find difficulty putting it down.

Micro sentences, are a content writers best friend. Little short stubby powerhouses. Anywhere from 1 to 5 words. Most effectively used near the end of a string of sentences. (More on that special technique later.) Use them at the beginning and end of a paragraph. Though, anytime is a good time for a micro sentence. It could easily become the most used creative writers trick.

The Challenge of beating out 249 ads.

Words must be more effective today, than at any time in history. Today, we have to compete against 36 billion dollars of advertising. Every year. That's online dollars only.

TV ads now comprise 32 percent of TV time. Our reader must value our words more than the other 249 ads they're confronted with each day. New York times once reported a figure that stands much higher. In their report we encounter 3,000 ads each day. Even more recently I've seen the figure of 2000 to 20,000 ads per day.

Either number drives the point in deep. Readers are saturated with marketing content. Their guard is up more than in the past. Our copy must embody excellence, to survive. **Getting in under their radar, is our only way to reach them.**

Shadow content, is a nearly unnoticed insertion of influential words and phrases. Word energy charged to capacity-- if you will. Covert expertise in writing calls for a new set of skills today. *This book* attempts to equip your message with that capability. Neural tuned copy relies on an element of stealth.

Stealth marketing like stealth fighters, can get through when other competitors crafts, are getting shot down. End over end they fall, in a fiery ball of burning copy. Right brain radar, which we learned about in Chapter Two takes out many of them. But that reader radar is rendered useless against undetectable covert copy. This is our mission. Get past our readers sales radar, and make a sale.

Though, it's not always about a sale is it? Maybe, sometimes, it's to touch the heart of our friend or relative with a moving message. Same difference, and same skill is required for both. Getting their brain to receive deeply our intended message.

The art of war. It's sometimes a matter of small wins. A paraphrase of Al Pacino from the feature film *"Any Given Sunday" (1999)* His locker room speech. I keep it, with many others on an MP3 player. Used for inspiration during workouts or difficult days. Or maybe when I'm down and finding it hard to push anymore. Eric Thomas, Sylvester Stallone, and a few others share the space on my MP3 player.

Here's Al's speech: *"Games are won by inches. Half a step to late and we don't quite make it. The inches we need are all around us".* Sure I'm aware of what you're likely thinking right now, I hear you. *" It's only a movie John".* Still, those statements are true. Heck, watching the Olympics shows us those statements are true.

One half of a second is long enough to change a life. One champion is decorated by a medal of gold, and the next morning he can join you for breakfast, as you're spooning a chilled bowl of Wheaties. The other not quite champion. Missed it by a sliver of a second, goes back to his job within a week. The football movie, played on that truth, to make the locker room moment more meaningful. More moving. If it wasn't true, they would have never used those lines in one of the greatest football movies every made.

The writers knew that the audience would recognize the reality of those statements. It's just a movie, yea--about real life. The art of war, can be a matter of *small* wins.

What's the most dangerous *beast* on the planet? It's killed more people than any other animal. **The mosquito**. Small, virtually undetectable and get's it done by stealth. Getting under the skin. We shouldn't underestimate small or stealth. What the...ouch! I think something just bit me..:-)

Suspense and Gospel Truth

According to one respected writing expert, short sentences create more **suspense**. I say, a chain of them can hit you like a rapid fire machine gun of thoughts. There's a writers saying which I believe was made more famous in a New York Times op-ed article by Roy Clark. It's not his saying, he just made it famous by attaching his own reputation to it. *"The five word sentence is gospel truth"*. Author Tom Wolfe, referred to that writer's truth according to Roy, after hearing a line of B.S. His point was this: **"If you have a preposterous message, say it in 5 words or less, to get the most credibility out of it."** His words not mine.

The respected Poynter Institute claims the title of "The leading educator of journalist worldwide" on it's website. I got no argument there. From their website, that same international writing coach, American writer and editor Roy Peter Clark, states, your most powerful sentences should be the shortest. He refers to that concept as *"slamming on the brakes"*. For an example of this, look at my *"The mosquito"* line, two paragraphs above.

Another master "America's most influential writing teacher" also wrote a book on the very subject of short writing. He calls short writing essential, for this internet age.

Our subconscious leaves open doors. Often times that door may be just big enough for a micro sentence to slip right in. Insert a micro sentence. Or two. Do it to start off a paragraph. Do it at the end of a string of sentences to **thrust home** your point.

Take-Away: Use a *Micro sentence* to put a punch in your main finishing points. It delivers powerful concluding impact. Use to start a new paragraph. It also makes an inviting welcome mat.

A three word movie?

A few simple words, have the power to trigger, full blown images in our mind.

In fact, I could paint a vivid picture for you in just two words. Grand Canyon. I'll create an independent attitude in two: *"Marlboro Man"*. Better yet, I will play a short movie in your mind with just three words. *"Make my day" (Dirty Harry)*. Maybe a love story, *"You complete me.." (Jerry Maguire)*. How about four words? *"Houston, we have a problem"(Apollo 13)*. If you want to pack a punch in your copy *"Go for it"(Rocky)*. It doesn't take many words. It takes the right words. Is it easy? NO. It takes far longer to come up with three powerful and perfect word droplets, than it does a river of dribble. (gross pun intended;-).

Eighteen

Micro sentence marketing.

"Snap Crackle Pop" wasn't easy. But it was right. In order to beat Reebok, ad man Dan Weiden came at them with *"Just Do it"*. In "doing it", Nike demonstrated the power of three common words. In fact, I'll bet you have a pair. I do. It's in the top three *"most memorable marketing lines in history."* (Hunsberger, 2008). Not bad for eight letters huh?

Shorter lines are easier to recall. Harder to argue with. Therefore they get in to the subconscious easier. They're less threatening. Simple to swallow. Create less resistance. Does size matter? Yep. Smaller is better in this case.

You might be asking yourself, why is smaller better? Well, I'll answer that. Do you like big hairy spiders? Which would you rather find crawling on you, a big hairy spider or a cute little ant? An ant of course. If I made a steamy pot of YUCK soup, and you were forced to take a spoonful, would your first bite be a big daddy sized bite, or a little baby size bite? A baby sized of course. That's because you're unsure of what it will taste like.

Your readers are on guard too. They have to be. They're trained to be. Trained by 36 billion dollars of annoying marketing content. If I can, I'm going to step out of myself and be cute for a moment. I'll return after this next line. Don't just write your copy, **right** your copy. Cute huh?

When we are on guard, we like small. We trust small more than big. Baby steps. Use the period. Liberally. Carve a longer sentence up and serve it in halves. Like mom did, with the peanut butter and jelly sandwich. Grammar, takes a back seat to compelling a reader or a customer. Making the sale or a point, comes before grammar in my copy.

There's a simple test to check you copy's sentence length. The average sentence length in this section of copy was eight words. You can calculate your own copy's average sentence length too. Use the Find tool, to find and replace the periods with the # sign. Click "replace all". It will then tell you how many periods it replaced. Then change it back. Use the "word count" feature to get the word count. Divide the words by the periods, to get your average sentence length.

Before we switch it up in Chapter Nineteen, I'm giving you some candy. Thought candy. It's the next two points. Taste so good to ponder, it feels like candy to your brain. We'll call it brain candy.

The *Magic* of less. Less is more.

Something occurs inside our brain when we see less. It triggers our imagination. One word book titles are among the hottest selling books. Why? Giving less, means the reader MUST engage their own imagination. It is involuntary. Our brain instinctually tries to solve our mysteries. That process also creates a feel good emotional reaction. We like to solve mysteries. Come on, admit it. You love a big juicy rumor. Don't you? It makes you wonder, what other secret doors the rumor may open up if this first one is true. That's your imagination, loving the rumor.

Too much information, shuts down the readers imagination. They don't need it. Hence--boredom. To engage the emotional regions in the brain, sometimes fewer words works better than more. Even to the extreme. One word.

What's your favorite song?

Think of a few of the lines in that song.

Can you think of the number of words in each phrase, of your favorite song?

Most songs, choose 3 to 4 words per line. Nothing moves me like a great song.

Small compact phrases can have the greatest impact on our mind and emotions.

Nineteen

The "Tall Sword" of Copy

(The long sentence and writing pictures)

Glimmering steel, hardened and stinging, sunk into a great stone. Long promised to the true king of copy, and only he dare uproot it. A keen-edged tool, for the astute writer of long copy. If this sword is for you, it shall pull out, if not, it remains.

As with the original *"Sword In The Stone" (White, 1938),* most who attempt this long sword writing technique, flounder. Short sentence is a sure thing. Long sentence is twice the risk, but for twice the treasure.

Lethal swords boast a double edge. In that quality, lies danger for its wielder. Two edges cut well, both ways. The long sentence is no different. It can inflict harm to the copy or preserve the warm crimson life blood within. As a general rule, the longer the sentence the more damage you can do with it. The reader can get spooked if not done well.

In the hands of a worthy swordsman, it's found conquering dramatic new virtual written worlds. It does well for visually descriptive sentences. Use it carelessly, and suffer the fate deserved of a careless swordsman.

Espoused proficiently, not one reader can repel its energy or its colorful theater of artistry. Behold, the *long sentence.*

There is one primary use for which the long sentence is unmatched.

Writing pictures.

One thing the long sentence does that a short sentence could never do--paint a vivid picture, into the mind's eye. This idea of **writing a picture**, is a real thing. Our brain generates mental images every day. From the hour we raise our lids bright, until the second we close those two doors and lock them, at night.

Reader becomes writer.

It's perfectly natural for the brain to brush a picture into our thoughts. As you may know, we observe with brain more than eye. Two advantages come with more words.

One, is the opportunity to describe imagery in greater flowing detail. A fair *image* is worth 1,000 words. But even a glimpse that blossoms emotion and picturesque story, takes on life itself. It's value? Maybe 10,000 words.

And two, the opportunity to hold that image in mid thought, suspended with no deterrent. Longer in mind, as the sentence continues on. Sustaining the image in time, giving added moments for imagination to build on it and enjoy it. To live within it.

Preserving the impression, affords a reader enhanced deepening of the scene. Inspiring reader elaboration. A ripening of the word fruit. The life it takes on, infuses the reader's own thoughts into the created world. *Reader becomes writer.*

Reader enhances the image to his own custom imagination. Based on his own life experience and memory. Seeing the word through the eyes of their own life. Theater through the *movie screen* of their own history and dreams. That is magic even a film, cannot achieve.

Movies impose some visual limitations, and suggestive visual interpretations. Boundaries where mind is not allowed access. Where as text or even a song does not impose great boundaries. A song allows more open and personal visual interpretation. Allowing listener to fill in the missing visuals, with their own version. Again seeing through the eyes of they're own life. Personal interpretation works just the s same way reading words.

Textual painting, unites writer and reader for a joint collaboration. Assembling a thought, requires time. The lengthened sentence does just that. Holds the thought, giving moments for the brain to touch, to paint, to experience. Time also allows their imagination to embellish on the newly born mental image. Personalizing it to suit their own desires and beliefs.

Compare these examples of the same sentence core, which has been extended slightly, each time. *Pause* for a few seconds after each reading. *Compare* them for 3 qualities.

One, the mental image they create in your mind.

Two, the length of time each one forces you to hold the image.

Three, the elaboration of thought which seeps in during that time, as the sentence grows longer. (That's the part which you compose it with your own imagination. It's where reader becomes writer.)

"I fell down." .... Pause....

" I tripped and fell down..... Pause...."

" I tripped on a stone, stumbled and fell down." .... Pause....

"I tripped on a tan jagged baseball size stone, stumbled like a drunk, and fell down hard in humiliation, as she walked by."......Pause....

The longer sentence should have brushed a more life like picture, allowing deeper emotional content to connect with you.

For myself, imagery is one of the most important exceptions for using long sentences. Creating a 3D image in a readers mind, is easier done with descriptive sentences. Which require more words. The payoff ,is giving the reader a vivid image to immerse themselves in. Fantasy novels use this technique a lot. Great writers can get a way with it easily, because our eyes are just devouring their words and want more of them.

The Land of words.

It's not that either length is right or wrong. Each word must earn it's keep though. The longer the sentence grows the heavier price we'll pay for adding more. If a sentence were land or real estate, the first few words would come cheap. No price to pay for using short sentences. No risk of losing a reader on a short sentence. Eventually as the sentence grows, the price we will pay for each word would never return our investment. The cost is memory decay, and overload which will burn the reader and you. Better to start a new line and get the word land cheap again.

Multi-dimensional messages.

Creating a multi-dimensional message can be done by loading it with sensory rich words and phrases. A second way is by adding this type of longer sentence, building *visual dimension.* Here's an example of how David Baldacci did it properly, in his book *The Finisher.*

"I decided to approach the cottage, not from the front or rear but from the right side" (Baldacci 2014)

As you re-read that line, notice how he cleverly drew a three dimensional cottage with words. In order for a reader to read the line, they must envision each side of the cottage separately, one at a time, as David mentioned it. Why did he have to mention three sides? Front, rear and right side. The character was only going to enter from the right side, so why didn't he just say that? The long sentence, slowly painted a cottage, mentioning each side as it's own image, giving the reader time to imagine it and build it with his mind. By the time the sentence was read, it was a full blown 3D scene.

The combination of using sensory rich words, and also painting a 3D picture, constructs a reality. Putting shape, color, scent, texture, sound, temperature and feeling to our copy. It's ALIVE! (not really, but in the readers mind it becomes a virtual reality).

Take-Away: Use *Longer sentence* to compose pictures and scenes. Spin visual and emotional moments. Create dimensional aspects using descriptive language. Depth, height, feel, color, scent, sound, movement, touch.

Twenty

How to build trust, (When they've never even heard of you).

As you know, **Trust** is a major component in successful marketing. March 25 2013, Watershed Publishing of Vermont, headlined an article *"Few People Trust Social Media Marketing,.."*. Cited in the article was a Forrester Research survey. It poled 75,000 adults in two countries. The results? 85% did not trust social media marketing. 90% distrusted ads on websites. 91% answered that text messages from companies, were untrusted. What *did* 70% of the crowd trust?

Opinions from from friends or family. They were the most trusted, at 70%. There was a second most trusted category. The runner up: **55% trusted professionally written online reviews**. These were trusted even more than consumer-written online reviews. So by now, you may by asking yourself, "What about email marketing?"

Here's where it gets even better. What's been called a *"bench marking"* report from another marketing research firm, reveals email marketing stats. Topping the list, **80% want relevant and compelling content.** Stop and think about that for a second. 80% of people agreeing on anything is huge. I'm sure you're aware that email marketing is the shiny golden grail of online sales. Statistically, an 80% chunk of our email list, sanely cannot be ignored. Not if we're committed to reaching them in our copy. Not if we want to have happy fans. Fans that offer to buy our dreams for us. So what's the takeaway?

The reader has spoken: **Relevant and Compelling** content is job ONE to them. Highest priority for 80% of our list. So how *do* we compel them? Not quite so fast.. There's a catch that will drive home the point to all these numbers. Here it is: 40% of marketers surveyed said CREATING RELEVANT and COMPELLING CONTENT was the most challenging thing for them to do.

Let's boil it all down to three simple facts. One, **people don't trust** online marketing. Two, people want **relevant and compelling** content. Three, those two things **are hard to fix.**

But what if there was a way to juice our content. A way to compel our readers. A way to win their trust.? (By the way, if a reader doesn't trust us, our content is by extension, less compelling, no matter what the offer is)

It's the *"chicken and egg"* and *"who's on first"* routine, rolled into one big marketing dilemma. It goes like this - It's hard to sell if you're not known and trusted, but hard to get known and trusted if you can't sell. Could that obstacle get any more opposing?

Yes, here's why. If our readers don't yet trust us, then our copy loses value. And you'll scratch your head wondering why they're not buying. It doesn't matter how good our offer is, if they don't trust us. You can't really increase trust by chopping the price either. Too cheap of a price can actually reduce trust. The exact same ad, offered to a trusting reader as opposed to a complete stranger, will have drastically different results. **Trusting readers** are more easily compelled.

Take-Away: Try to establish trust early on in the message. Everything else we have to say or offer, hinges on trust. Trust pre-framing gives advantage to the rest of our message.

Twenty One

How to politely <u>force</u> a reader to Trust you and agree with you..

(In a nice way)

Here's how to fix all that, in 3 easy steps.

Trust Level One: The best way to get them to trust you, is to **force them to agree with you.** Sounds crazy at first. But I'm serious. It really works. I could force you to agree with me right now (in fact I already have), but I won't get into that just yet. I'll show you how first.

There's a way you can do it, with out them knowing they've been forced. It's not the violent type of force. It's more like that Star Wars type of Force. It should be done, right off the bat. Early in the message. Because everything else we have to say, depends on them trusting what we're saying. So how can we force a complete stranger to agree with us?

Easy. It's done by **stating things you both agree on.** Any fact, will do. Though it's better to use facts, related to your subject. This is called by some hypnotist a form of building rapport. Subliminally, it's a matter of quickly **training your reader that what you say, is fact.**

It's getting them used to agreeing with you. It's associating truth with your words. If you say three statements and they're all fact. Guess what? They'll have increased confidence that your 4th statement will follow the same pattern. It all takes place under the surface. It's covert. They don't know they're being trained to trust you. But they are.

Create a pattern of thought. You state a fact, they must agree. Because it's fact. Repeat. You state, they agree. Once they start to believe your words ,then they ease up on not trusting you. They start to accept what you say as trust worthy. You gain credibility. It stops them from scrutinizing your copy without reason. At that point you've disarmed them.

Now you can begin to present your other targeted content or offer related messages. The spotlight is off of the trust issue, and more directed at your message quality. Which will be less likely to get falsely red flagged by their B.S. meter.

The trick is to do this at the very top of your copy or story. There's a reason why it must be done first. Because if they don't agree and trust you, then it doesn't matter what else you say. They won't believe it as much. If they don't trust you, then your words lose value. So does your offer and products.

Take a few lines to just build their confidence. Here's an example: *"As you know, internet marketing is a crowded field. Wiki answers, suggested there are 20,316,218 online marketers strong"* . I've just stated two facts, which are indisputable.

Another example: *"October 27 1997 the Dow Jones crashed 554 points. Just 2 years later, the dot.com boom skyrocketed the market."* Immediately I'm put in a different light because of those facts. After reading a few of your facts. They start to associate your words, with facts. Subconsciously. A wise man believes what is most probable. If you spoke twice and both were facts, then the third time will have earned a bit of pre-trust before you ever speak it.

This technique establishes thought patterns. Each time we state a fact, their guard is lowered a bit more. We're establishing credibility. Credibility creates agreement. What's at stake in trust? Our very dreams. And hopefully our readers dreams as well.

Take -Away: For *Trust*. Force the reader to agree with you early on, by stating some facts.

Trust level Two - Authority

Step two: **Establish dominance.** By dominance I mean authority. In the world of hypnosis, they use similar preparation techniques. It's called **authoritative strategies.** Any command will do. A hypnotist (which I am not) may say, "Hold out your hand", or "tilt you head back a bit, and relax", or "just relax and think of a day at the beach". Or "Count to 10 for me". Maybe , " Have a seat". Hypnotists state a command, which their subject would comply with. They comply purely on reflex.

Subconsciously they are acknowledging *authority*, by submitting. Submitting to the person giving the command, which under the surface, establishes authority. We learn this as kids, from out parents and teachers.

The idea, is that once we've established authority, they will be more likely to comply with our call to action as well.

Of course, only to a degree, but it helps. It reduces the inclination to resist. As a bonus benefit, they will also feel **compelled to trust you.** People trust authority generally. The key is to do it in a kind way, an interesting way. Not a bossy way.

In writing, that could be done by stating things such as: *"Think back to a time when you were a kid. What is it , that was most important to you then?"* Telling them to think back, is a command. A subtle instruction which they will obey, purely by reflex.

The first time you do it, precedence it set. More than once and you've created a pattern of behavior. Patterns or habits, tend to be repeated. Once established, it could theoretically help their motivation in your call to action. Directly impacting conversions. Above all though, it relates to trust.

Another example of writing a command: *"You might want to grab a pen and paper, for the important parts I'll cover in this webinar."*

Okay, remember in the first chapter I mentioned that you've just be brain-hacked? Remember this?: *(FYI: you've just been brain-hacked, I'll explain later;-)* It's later. The paragraph above this one, explains the hack that I used on you in Chapter One. Which was this *" Grab a pen and a notebook for your favorite points."*

Those are covert commands which can subconscious establish authority. Only the super Ninja copywriters use them or even know about them.

Here's another example: *"Stop and think for a minute, of how many people before you, have succeeded in this business."* Those type of examples do not sound threatening. They don't sound like a command, but they are.

They will not be detected as commands, which makes them extremely effective. These are subconsciously directed commands. They establish authority without the reader realizing it. Before long, you are gaining interest in your trust account. Now, here's the third level of trust.

Take -Away: For *Trust,* establish authority covertly. Introduce polite commands. Be cool about it though.

Twenty Two

Association (The trio of trust).

Trust Level Three: Association. This third method is fairly easy too. The obvious method that most are familiar with is fairly blatant. Just get your picture taken with a celebrity and instantly, you're one too. So if Tom Cruise is your best friend, by all means go that route. My way is for those of us who can't get a hold of Tom when we need him. Or maybe there's a few of you that don't know him at all. So the Tom method is out for most. If you do know him them you're probably already a celebrity and can skip to the next chapter.

Still here? Me too... What is it we like to have on our eggs? Hint: it's shaken not stirred. (No, not a martini... you party way too much:-) Answer: Salt and Pepper.

 The the original "Old Spice" classic pair, is known as *"compositional association"* . According to the really smart science guys, it means they maintain their individuality but still remain associated together.

 If either one of them is setting on your stove, I'll make a sizable wager, that that other is sitting right beside it. One is not viewed as supreme over the other, or of a higher class. They're both just everyday spices. The idea of associations we're interested in, is when the two are of different classes. It can be a little tougher and more valuable.

Three things are involved to get a good associative memory stored. It relies on three ways our brain stores information. Here they are - *meaning, imagery* and *sound* (sound can mean talking). After those three, the finishing touch is hammering them home with a little repetition.

 First to do is *meaning.* It's the word or name itself of a person or thing that we want to be associated with, in our copy. Now this part is crucial and has one special requirement. It has to have some sort of logical connection to you. It has to make sense in some way for the brain to give it true associative *meaning* and store it as such. (Other wise it's stored as B.S. and it will infect the trust you've have already gained.)

For example. If it's a person we want association with, then we should have some level of commonality such as, friendship, business involvement, alliance, both have the same car, we use their products, they use ours, something that makes some level of a logical connection to you. A real *meaning*. There must be some real reason for saying it.

Secondly, is to create a mental *image* of association with the word or person. The best type of word *image* to create is a 3D image. Like a real life shape. (Discussed in Chapter Nineteen.) Do this by language that refers to dimension, depth and color. This step relies on a special part of the brain. It's referred to as *"the mind's eye"*. This eye, is our brain's ability to visualize mental *imagery.*

Remember our brain actually generates the images we think we are seeing with our eye. Our eye really doesn't see the things we look at. It see's information and gives it to the brain which then creates the image, in our head. So generating *images* from other data such as words, is also possible. Once the image is created by the brain, it's saved and it's then retrievable, from our memory.

Ever seen the memory champs on TV perform incredible memory feats? Imagery association is one of the ways they are able retrieve their info. It's sometimes called V.A. Visualization Association. So it's a real thing. It enhances the readers ability to believe and remember.

As writers, we're just helping our reader use that same V.A. memory trick. We do it by force feeding the *image* into the readers memory (By *"force"*, I mean plant.).

***Sound* is the third step.** As the reader is reading the text, their internal voice is also classified by the brain as sound. It goes to the same part of the brain as if you were talking audibly face to face with them. This was highlighted earlier in Chapter Nine.

Brian Pasley of Neuroscience Research Lab at Berkeley mentioned on *"Through the wormhole"* with Morgan Freeman, that our brains internalized thoughts activate the same places in our brain, that audible language does. Saying that we actually do hear the voices.

The statement you are about to read, is not from a scientist. More surprising than that, it's not even from a college graduate. In fact, the statement I'm about to share with you, is not even from a high school graduate.

Hand printed on paper, by a 7 year old child is a response to his teacher. Explaining how he arrived at a math solution. Related to a problem the teacher had given. *"I got the answer by talking in my brain and I agreed of the answer that my brain got."*

Take that teach! Even children it seems, are aware of the voice in their head. It would be the same voice Brian Pasley of Berkely stated that we indeed can hear. The same voice our readers *brains* classify as audible. A photograph of the child's printed response was published on Yahoo news, in March of 2014.

Speaking of that (no pun intended there..it just blurted out all by itself. But I'm sort of glad it did:-). Have you a favorite singer? Guy or Girl it doesn't matter for this fun exercise. Think of a cool song that you love to sing to, by that singer.

Bring the song up in your head. Pulling them it up, something we all do, almost every day I suppose. Take a moment and get your internal jam on. Can you hear it? Now bring up your worst singer. (I got my worst in mind, but I won't mention his name. Initials are M.B.). Take a few seconds and listen to it. By doing that, what you just heard, both times, was brain generated. Cool huh?

We love to play these songs in our head. Why? Maybe because we really can hear them. It's awesome. So awesome, we (By we, I mean "I") occasionally start signing them out loud even.. When we think nobody can hear us. Or see us. My voice sounds slightly worse than one of those singing dogs we see on youtube. Doesn't stop me though. When I'm feeling the song, it's coming out, and with passion! Lord help us...

In the same way, the readers brain "hears" his internal voice as sound. And *sound* is one of the important ways our memory stores things. You're not going to believe this. But now, I want to go play some music. Seriously. I'm going to stop typing and play some music. See ya..

***

Now I'm back... dude, it's all real!

"Collide" by Howie Day and a few others. That's what I popped in me ear.

Fourthly take this step. The aspect of repetition. Once the image is created by text, it's best to recall it [in our copy] within 30 seconds of the first mention. It's held in our short term "working" memory up to 30 seconds. Mention it again later if possible.

Repetition is believed to be a key basis in longer term memory storage. Making it also retrievable in the future. Without memory, there would be no such thing as time. Our brain uses it's memory to distinguish past from present. If the reader has got it, why not use it? It's a powerful tool that a potent messages will tap into. So Basically it works like this.

I drop a name of something everyone knows and likes. Let's use something safe such as the *"Rocky Mountains"*. I put it in my copy. In mentioning it I try to paint a 3D word picture. The best way to do all this is in a story form.

Like, *"Made our first hike in the Rocky Mountains last week. The trail up the left side was too steep, we chose to approach it from the right. It took us 2 hours to reach the tree line, but we could see a postcard view of at least 100 miles, once we arrived. Air was a little thin but fresh and clean. One solitary chirping bird was the only wildlife we saw."* So now the image is planted.

Then later in my copy I use the word again, which forces them to recall the image and the association. *"After 4 hours of Kansas highway, I was missing the Rockies again."*. Done. The more I use it the more it gets joined in their memory to me.

In your copy, align yourself with trustworthy sources. Even the mere mention of a known trusted or liked name. (Like when I mentioned Star Wars earlier in this work). Sounds silly, but our brain really does try to fit things together for us. To help us. If I say something like "five karat diamond", your brain will instantly try to figure out why I said it. It tries to fit pieces of the puzzle together. To establish a connection.

Hearing or seeing something people already identify with or respect or like, in our copy, will add trust to our identity. It's a subliminal, under the radar technique. It's a subconscious association. It's not something that should be overtly evident like name dropping. That's just lame, and their right brain might flag it as B.S. or ego. If that is the case, then it will have the exact opposite effect. Remember, the right brain is a B.S. meter, and it works great. Right brain radar would destroy that type of lame attempt and our message. Before it ever get's to the readers brain. Be cool about it. Be real.

For example, a simple mention of the word Hollywood, sends all sorts of neural signals instantly to our brain from past associations we've had (now also connected in some small degree with my copy). Our brain automatically links them together. You can't stop it. If done using other emotional triggers mentioned, it will get planted in their memory. Hollywood memories, emotions, desires, stars, glitter, and lifestyle, all come crashing in just by hearing that word. It happens quietly and in a flash, but it happens, and doesn't just go away in a flash either. It's how words on our brain work. We can't stop it from happening. Here's why it works.

Our mind automatically tries to fill in the blanks. Fit pieces together. In fact, I feel the most powerful to say something, is not to say it at all. Imply it. Let the reader convince themselves it's true.

Our mind as you know, tries to find associations in order to make sense of our world. Making us more efficient thinkers and better at solving problems. It's why we can view a set of words that are missing some letters, and our brain still reads them, just fine. I'm sure you've seen that example before. It's filling in the blanks for us. Putting the pieces together.

Knowing that, we have a new tool to strengthen our copy. It's one more building block to keep in stock, for just the right fit. Associations can be direct, implied or indirect such as Star Wars was.

Also it's interesting to remember that our subconscious, is what makes most of our decisions, whether we know it or not. So once a thought is planted, that "data" becomes part of their thought process. Let's shift gears, and maybe head west. There's a question I've been wanting answered. But first I have a bonus.

Take-Away: For *Trust,* use *Associations.* Three step association method is: ***Logical*** connection to you, create a textual ***3D image*** description of the association, ***recall*** it within 30 seconds of read time. Hammer it home with repetition. Use story form to deliver the message. Meaning, imagery, sound and a hammer.

A Bonus for you.

Now for the Bonus. Yep, I'm giving you a bonus. It's not a bonus of inflation vulnerable cash. Oh no. And not a bonus of material possession, which as you know, has weakened even the strongest of men. Oh no. And not a bonus of gold or silver, which as you know, has sunk many a vessel. Oh no. You're far to wise at this point, to settle for those temporary bonuses. Aren't you? I said, aren't you? Oh alright, I don't blame you. But your not getting one of those anyway, so you might as well be grateful for the one I am going to give you..:) It's a bonus of *wisdom*...

This is the absolute most powerful, king of the ring, iron clad method, to build trust from a reader or customer--that anyone has ever used. It would benefit marketers for sure, but really anyone that wants to win trust of a reader. What is it? It's one word.

That's right just one word. And your mother, she's going to be very proud of you if you get it right... It's KINDNESS. Yep, *kindness* will drown the right brain in compassion. Instantly.

It'll transform your reader into a ball of soft, warm, putty. Complete strangers will succumb to it's power. Bad ass bikers, and skeptical readers the like. Some shrewd marketers link onto it slightly, when they employ the law of reciprocation. They give free gifts, or free content. Though that's just the para-scope, peeking above the surface of the water. Underneath is a massive submarine. A submarine that most marketers and copywriters don't even know is there. It's huge, and powerful to use.

A much larger force is available, than just free gifts. The strongest words in the English language are *"I'm sorry"* and *"Thank you"*. **Nobody can look down on a person that speaks either one sincerely.**

Ask yourself this question. When people write "thank you", where is it usually placed at? The end of a message, right? Directly above where you type your name.

When in fact, the most effective place to put it, is on your first line! By thanking them for something right off the bat, everything you state after that will be viewed with a humble spirit. *"I'm sorry"* works the same way. When we write in a humble tone, our readers hearts are engaged. Trust doesn't have to be something we prove, or earn. It can be something our readers **just decides to grant us**. Voluntarily.

By speaking to them from a humble place, they will want to treat you with respect too. Respect them, and they will respect you. Try it, and you'll be amazed at the change in the reader/writer relationship that occurs. Use them in the first line or two of your copy. Remind them again at the end.

Now, I said the bonus was not a monetary type. However, you will find very few techniques, if any at all, which pay off better than *Kindness*. Increased clicks, increased responsiveness, increased sales. It has worked since the beginning of time, and will work until the end.

Take-Away: Use *"Thank You"* and *"I'm sorry"*, sincerely. Other kindness works too. They work well in the first line or two of your copy. It earns you respect and trust. Humble yourself and they will too.

Twenty Three

Clones, Moods and Conversion. (From the lab to your message)

Would two human clones interpret the same copy in the same way?

Imagine if you will, this hypothetical scenario. If you had a clone, and I handed both of you a print out. Each of you had the exact same email copy offer to read. Would you expect your brain and your clones, to experience the same thoughts while reading the copy?

September 07, 2012 Stanford News published an article on a study. It involved multiple neurobiological (dang that's another big ole word) experts, radiologists and humanities scholars (Not quite sure what a humanities scholar is, but it sounds serious). With reddish brown hair and a bright red dress, researcher Natalie Philips points at some brain images on the screen

She's used eye tracking and neural imaging devices. The tested volunteers were given specific reading instructions. This machine they used, looks like it's ten feet tall. If it ever breaks down, they're is still one use for it. They could put it along side a Nevada highway as the worlds largest doughnut. Because that's about what it looks like. Natalie appears as a small child standing next to it. One volunteer lays out on the table being fitted with an eye tracking device. If it were a doughnut, the volunteer's head would be stationed right where the doughnut hole is.

They were given Jane Austen books to read. Jane Austen has amazing writing if you ever get a chance to enjoy it. Here's how the test went.

During one part of the test they read the book specifically **as if they were studying for an exam**. Then when a little green light turned on, **they read leisurely, purely for pleasure.** Allowed to skim as they might do in a book store. So, when they got the signal, the volunteers would supposedly change their frame of mind. My question is this: How do we know they actually changed their frame of mind? The study would seem to depend on our confidence that these volunteers did change their frame of mind on cue.

What they found, was important for copy writers. They discovered that *"our cognition is shaped not just by **what** we read, but by **how** we read it. "* Changing their attention from "study like" to "pleasure reading" had a big impact on their pattern of brain activity.

Pleasurable frame of mind increases the activity in the brains pleasure areas.

This is another one of those moments, in your life that you just heard a pivotal truth. Smoke it in. It will revolutionize your content's reach into the readers brain. Remember the "Association" take -away about Kindness? This pleasurable state of mind, taps into that same mode of mental processing. The brain just opens up for it.

What does this mean for us copywriters and marketers? A happier reader will see our copy in a more positive light. I'll cover that specifically, in just a few more paragraphs. A readers frame of mind, affects their interpretation of copy they read.

It changes the breadth of brain activity. As it turns out, the volunteers were all PHD candidates. So we can assume they weren't just a bunch of screwballs messing with Natalie's head. In other words, they probable really did change their frame of mind on cue. Making the test more reliable for us to believe.

So your clone, depending on his <u>mood</u> or relaxed state, may not activate the same parts of the brain as you, when reading. Pleasure center parts versus factual language parts. Even though you're both reading the exact same email copy. Unless your moods are identical, the copy could be interpreted differently. We are in the thick of it. This stuff too covert for covert. It's more like super covert tactics. I'm talking dark ops, invisible man stuff.

So how can that knowledge **help us make more money and convert better**?

Here's how: Keeping our reader in a good relaxed mood, will increase activity in their brain's pleasure regions. In fact putting our reader in a good mood has to be JOB ONE to maximize sales. It's called pre-framing. Pre-framing, is a covert method of setting the emotional stage in the readers mind. Using copy to firstly optimize their frame of mind. Before delivering our primary message or offer. Well how do I do that John, you may ask?

Starting your copy off with a "Thank you" or "I'm sorry" or some other form of kindness is the first step.

Is your our copy filled with facts and offers, but less story, curiosity, and sensory rich language? Build some emotional characteristics into your copy. Add some humor, or suspense to activate the minds pleasure zones. Think of it like warming the car up on a cold morning.

Skip that part and you might be driving away without the reader. Even if he does come with you, they'll leave their wallet at home. No emotional content and we're boring the brain to distraction. Because only the factual part of their brain would be engaged -- that's Lefty.

After you warm up the car with emotional triggers and hit the road, then go ahead and put the top down, because you got <u>convertible</u> copy! As in -- able to convert. (Little play on words there... I'm trying very hard to control my brain "humor region" :-)

In the fall of 2011, way over there, at Hove England, something interesting was published in the Journal of Cognitive Psychology. The article which birthed this snippet, has been cited over 25 times. *"...emotional stimuli tend to capture our attention more easily than non-emotional stimuli, and thus may affect different levels of our cognition.....(e.g., better memory for emotional events) "* (Dolcos 2011)

Let me trim the fat and slice you off a piece of what the science guy just served up. Hand me your plate. **Emotional words get processed faster and remembered longer**, than neutral words. Shabaam!

He then piled that meaty dish even higher. Some of these memories apparently produce long term effects --*"lasting a lifetime"*. Now, speaking for myself, I would love my readers, friends and people to which I provide a service or product, to remember me for a lifetime.

You for instance. If ten years from now you're still using the assets I've shared with you here in my book, and banking serious coin from it, then it would rock.

Because, if we're not making someone else's life better, then we're wasting our time. Care for second helpings anyone? *" Studies of memory <u>retrieval</u> also showed that emotional memory is particularly resilient to time, ... up to 1 year..."*

It means we can grab it anytime we want, easily up to a year later. So, embedding our message into our readers brain, might best done through emotionally rich copy. Bring it in here, group hug:-) Plant the message well, fertilized with emotional content, and it may stay green for an entire year, or even a lifetime.

If I want my reader to eagerly read my copy and keep thinking about it afterwards, I have to make an emotional impact on them. If all I make is an offer, or share facts, my copy would scientifically suck.

Take Away: Use e*motional* content to create a relaxed mood in the person reading. A readers relaxed state of mind, activates more brain regions (i.e more engaged reader). Emotional content, gets our message processed faster (because it's given a higher priority) and it's remembered longer. Up to 1 year, and kept in storage up to a lifetime.

Twenty Four

Does your copy sport a happy face or a sad face? (Or a poker face?)

How important is the "face"of our message?

Professor Lisa Barrett at Northeastern University, has shown in studies, a quite interesting result. When people saw facial expressions relating to joy or happiness, they tended to interpret other images in light of that happy emotion they had just viewed.

For example, I show you two pictures at the same time, side by side. One is a smiling person. The other picture is virtually an unrecognizable mesh of patterns. Just an incomprehensible unclear picture. When people see those two pictures side by side they usually think the unrecognizable picture is something happy or positive too. (Because the happy face they just viewed, is influencing their perception.)

On the other hand, when a frowning or angry face is shown next to the same unclear picture, people usually think the unclear picture is something negative.

Okay, in your brain right now, you should be hearing the word Shabaam! Even though I held back and didn't say it. This simple little test, is like the the difference between knowing gravity is real, or not. Copy that ignores this mood association principle, has missed the opportunity leverage emotion. Neural tuned high performance copy must have a happy face.

In other words, if I'm feeling happy, or seeing happy, I am more likely to interpret an unclear object or a word or phrase in a way that conforms to my feeling of happiness. In my view it could be another behavior of pre-framing tendencies that occur in the readers mind. The stuff we see, and words we read are interpreted to some degree, according to what else the reader is seeing or feeling at the time. This discovery has incredible implications for increasing sales and response results in copy.

In another study, a completely different kind of test was given to about 35 people. This study had actors read a line of jibberish. Not real words.

Five different times they read. Each time they were told to present a different mood. Same line, different mood. To inject an attitude in their reading presentation. Five reads, each with a different mood. The words they read, sounded real but were actually not real words at all. Actors made five different readings. Each spoken in a different way. With changes in tonal ques and mood, such as sadness, anger, joy, relief or a neutral emotion.

So we can see the similarities in the premise of this study compared to Lisa Barrett's studies above. Both used unrecognizable presentations. (Lisa's used visual, and this second study used verbal). Both are gauging the volunteers interpretation. Their perception. Both based on mood or attitude.

Using brain imaging on the listeners, they found a surprising result. Would the findings contradict Lisa's Northeastern studies mentioned above, or confirm them? Place your bets...

The listeners brain scans showed, that with every different mood the actors portrayed while reading the same line, a different signature was left on the brain. Remember, they were the SAME lines read each time. Just different mood or tone. Even though the same exact words were read the brain reacted differently. **Your copies mood**, affects your sales, clicks and reader engagement.

This seems to strengthen the first unrelated study above. (At least in my mind) If the brain reacts differently to the same sentence, read in a different way, then that could mean one of two things. At least to me.

Of course, if you're in a different mood than me, they may mean something different to you... just kidding....sort of:-) Here's the two things I think it could reveal. Either the tone itself caused the brain to categorize the line with a unique mood meaning. Or the tone itself first changed the emotions of the listener, which then caused a potentially different reaction in interpreting the lines. (Because the listener's mood was changed by the tone or mood of the reader).

As see it, either the listeners brain reacted differently because of what it heard, or the readers mood changed first, which made their brain react differently. Either way, the results are powerful.

Either way, *emotions*, changed the brains response.

That's what counts to me. Results were published in an issue of Current Biology, and a write up was posted on abc news HealthDay online. The study was performed by Swiss scientists. Other studies I've read, have shown that positive emotions have increased cognitive function. In light of the two just mentioned here, that would hit me as sensible.

In fact, according to researchers the easiest emotion to recognize using fMRI imaging was the *happiness* emotion. That particular finding is very recent. Though it arrived with yet another unexpected twist.

The emotions were sometimes only experienced on a subconscious level. Hmmm. They felt it alright, without knowing they were feeling it.

The brain changed, without the reader being consciously aware it had changed.. Way cool. Why is that important for us, as copywriters of the future?

Well, these writing hack concepts are specifically designed to hand deliver signals, straight to that unconscious language level. It means, even if the readers are not aware of the "shadow content", they are still being affected by the emotional triggers we send in. Making a dual language writing system like *you are learning now*, that much more effective. The study was reported in Science Daily, but occurred at Carnegie Mellon University.

Our emotions "contextual environment" is the background of textual settings, we create. It influences the readers perception of the copy. Writing a happy, sad or straight faced copy could affect the impact our message gives a reader. Also affecting our call to action results. It influences the meaning of our messages. So how can we use this science to build a better relationship with a reader? To influence them more? To convert and sell more?

Create a positive, happy emotion in a reader and they could be more likely to perceive what you say in that positive light. For a marketer, that could translate to more clicks. In general though, any reader would like our message more, if we put them in a good mood first. That's what the studies suggest.

To do that tactically, take the reader on a hilly ride. Ups and downs. To make them feel happy, sometimes it helps to rise from a lower place. Elation might be achieved by rising from a place of the opposite emotion. The sky never seems bluer than after several days of rain and clouds. Right?

The emotional ups and downs of a great story, peak our emotions in a stronger way, than by just presenting one constant side of an emotion. More details on that when we talk **Stories,** starting after one more chapter. By influencing the readers emotional ride, we can influence how well they **receive** our copy. It may influence their choice, to roll out the welcome mat or not -- for an offer or call to action.

Take-Away: By stimulating the readers happy emotions, we can influence *where* their brain sends the message. It determines how well they receive it, altering perception of our copy, offer, and call to action. They interpret messages, based on the particular *emotional* slant we give it.

Twenty Five

Rainy days and old movies.

Drift back for a moment. Do you recall those cloudy drizzling days, where all you wanted to do was curl? Just cozy up and watch a good movie or read a book? Those overcast mornings or afternoons made us feel sort of melancholy. Maybe having a hot bowl of comforting soup sounded extra special? Play a sad song and follow your memories far and away. Do the gray overcast days, cause you to be more reflective? Bringing to mind a loved one you may have lost and missed. Or maybe just hanging out inside seemed more fun than being outside.

In comparison, pull up in mind those other types of days. Waking up after several non stop days of rain or clouds, opening the door and getting slapped in the face by a bright blue sky. That's the good kind of slap. Step one foot outside, then another. The clean air smells pure and invigorating. Your emotions, motivation and inspiration just can't wait to get out there and enjoy it. Ride your bike, walk your dog named Charlie or Butch or Winston or Cesar or whatever you decided to name your furry friend. Wash the car, cruise to the park. Anything to get outside and just be a part o it.

And when you do, something has changed -- everyone else is outside too. The sidewalks are busy with dog-walkers and joggers. Bike riders and shoppers are all about. Why?

What changed? Why do we respond differently just because brightness of the day changed? The colors the smells, they seem to trigger everyone as a call to action would. A call to get busy, get inspired, live. Notice how when the environment changes, people change their thoughts and decisions?

Plans are made, activities take top priority and motivation is abounding. This is the power of our right brain, when it's senses are stimulated and engaged. Those senses, sight, sound, touch and smell change how we perceive our world. And what we read.

With positive *stimuli* our choices change and we're more motivated. Always wanted to use that word "stimuli". It kinda sucked though. Looks like it's missing a letter or two. Not to worry, I won't use it again. "Stuff" is better.

According to AccuWeather a study was done in 2008. It showed *".. The less sunlight people were exposed to, the more they exhibited depression-like symptoms"*. Weather engages our senses. Our senses affect how we perceive our world--including reading copy. Here's a question. Is it just weather that can change our mood and our outlook on life?

The same copy as we just saw, could be perceived in different ways, depending on the copy environment it is read in. Also depending on the mood of the reader, as we learned in a previous chapter. The readers mood, can be enhanced by nudging those emotional reflexes.

By deliberately writing a happy, sad or straight faced copy we suit our primary message or call to action. There could be a perfect time for each one. And a wrong time. Even the colors on the page itself affect the feel of the copy. Ebook covers they say, impact book sales now, by 50%. What does that mean for us message writers?

Date much?

Imagine a romantic dinner you've had in mind all year. A dinner you had planned to pop the question. Arriving at the restaurant, instead of candles, you're surprised to see lights blaring on you like an operating room. Dated decor clashing. Remember when I asked you to recall your worst singer? Imagine your worst singers song piping out of the speakers loudly. You know, like an early morning punch in the face.

Your waiter, he's sporting a stained Hawaiian shirt and sandals. Even if the food is great, will it matter at this point? You turn around and notice your date is now three steps behind you... Uncertain whether the next step they place, will be toward the car, or deeper into this pit of pain. How would that setting affect the message you had intended on sending to your love?

Being sensitive to the dual level message we are presenting, develops the *complexion* of our copy. Because we are delivering a dual message whether we know it or not. Our job is the make the duality complement each other.

Colors matter, feel matters, clutter matters, confused copy matters, quantity and quality both matter. Colors that don't shock or disrupt the message's mood could help the message be received. Right brain is stimulated by mood, and has to enjoy the read too. Or it may rebel.

Right brain and left brain are on a date. Your copy is the restaurant. What will their experience be like? If one is turned off, they both head for the car..

The *emotional color* of the message affects the readers mood too. Which in the end, affects how they perceive our message. It affects their purchasing and clicking decisions too.

The *context* of our primary message, could have a fortune to do with how that primary message or call to action will be sensed. **Perception changes the message.** Like rain or shine for your message. Like a bright blue sky can spark your energy. Or a cloudy day can zap it. Perception can be influenced by creating the right emotional environment.

The three best selling eBooks on Amazon, have one thing in common. Mystery and suspense. (well umm..that's two things...not one. So I screwed up. Oh well, it's too much work to go back and change all those words. I mean, I am way behind schedule on this book, every extra letter I have to type, just puts me that much further behind. Anyway, the two things are related..right? So it's kinda' like one word, almost.:-)

The million-dollar eBook author, Amanda Hocking is a master of that skill. On February of 2011 young Amanda was written up in USA today. Young, rich and shoots directly at those emotional targets. From the outside cover to the last page. Why do readers, buy her books, over and over? Why are mystery slash suspense slash fantasy books on the top 3 Amazon best sellers? One word. Emotions. They stir em'.

They deliver an emotional and sensory rich experience. We could do the same. Ignite sales, with a powerfully blended message and environment.

Take-Away: Setting up the e*nvironment* and state of our reader, to fit the message, will unite right and left brain senses. Fun, excited or curious states are also pleasurable states. A pleasurable relaxed state increases brain activity while reading. Create a sensory rich environment with our colors and general feel of our copy. One that suites the primary message or offer.

Well you did it! Cars are all washed and waxed. Deck is sanded. Fence is painted. The hard part is done. Arms might be soar, but you posses some lethal writing instincts now. *"Danielson! Show me paint the fence!"* (Karate Kid -Kesuke Miyagi).

Great movie, that still inspiring many years later. This was quite a few new concepts but we got through them. After 25 chapters of writing hack secrets I hope you've got some new assets that can be used, **forever.**

You know the how and the why. The next chapter starts the process of teaming them up. You know what they say: *"One stick by itself is quickly snapped, but a bundle tied together, is not easily broken."*

Twenty Six

Okay, we've laid out a few hand fulls of building block concepts of neural-tuned writing hacks. Now here's how they're used, as a <u>team</u>.

(How to unite a message with story.)

A Story machine. Story is the part that ties all the principles together. Before we cut into the heart of the reader, we need to cut into the heart of our copy body. I'd like to share some basic drama theory Yep, it's a real thing too... I know, I looked it up :-). Because story is all about emotional drama. Screen writers use this very stuff to construct their plots. Plots empowered to deliver epic drama to millions. The movies you embrace the most, have those very elements designed into their core structure. By intention.

My eyes were excited to come on these simple, life giving forces infused into great drama. Whenever I see them blended into movies, it repeatedly reminds me of the power they carry. Let's face it, we all love drama or there would be no such thing as the Academy Awards.

At least we'd never have heard of them. To give the bigger picture of *Story*, let's break open these few simple concepts.. For me it's much easier to grasp, if I know where things might fit in. To the big picture. The interconnection of things, paints a larger, easier picture to understand. One made easier to discern. If I understand how things work together, then I truly understand the mechanism.

My first business ever I owned, was an HVAC and appliance service company. To succeed at that, it required to understand disassemble and repair a lot of stuff. I mean a LOT of stuff. Every brand, of every year, of every type, of furnace, air conditioner and major house hold appliance. Being able to take it completely apart and put it back together. (And still work.)

It made my already analytical mind, even more analytical. That's a lot of machines to know how to fix. It could have taken a lot of memory. What made it possible for me, was first seeing how each part of a machine interacted with the other. Once I knew this, every single part had a *purpose* and I could easily remember what it was.

By attaching a purpose, to each part I understood the machine as a whole. Then I could diagnose most problems in just seconds. Memory without purpose, is a strained effort. At least for my brain. Uniting purpose to the little pieces, brings a complex process down to an easy level--My level :-)

This idea of all the individual building blocks, fitting into a bigger story *"machine"*, is the idea here.

This story section will put a purpose to all those individual conceptual building blocks we just covered in the past 25 chapters.

The stories you create for your readers, will do the same for them. It will give a stronger purpose for your offer and help the reader remember all the little facts and pieces you told them about. Some of best marketing copywriters I've seen, such as Frank Kern, are master story tellers. It could be the secret sauce.

Great story it's said, is often based on a few basic, easy to remember principles. The same principles were used in film to create Hollywood's mega-icon stars.

The six writing weapons of great story.

At the center is the character. Then add five other ingredients. *Conflict, consequences, stakes, countdown* and *quantity* of people affected. That combination is the *ready mix* story, in a box. A story cake. All movies (almost) are built around those five elements.

A *character* is the main part. The character *is* the story. (You or your product will be the main character.)

The *conflict* or *challenge* defines the character. Their values, strengths and weaknesses. We need to know those, to appreciate the challenges the character will face.

The *stakes* for failure and for success add drama. The higher the stakes, the greater the drama. As long as it's believable.

The *quantity* of people each challenge will affect adds more drama. A story that only impacts the main character might lack leverage that could have added more emotional teeth.

The *Villain*. Introducing an opposing character, with an opposite agenda and heavy stakes for that character, adds even more drama.

Introducing deadlines like a *countdown*, which adds pressure, also escalates drama. **That's the story basics.** Not too bad huh?

The story can start with revealing some of the values of the main character. Then a problem or *challenge i*s the next step. It's the most common way at least. Whether it's just a quick paragraph story or an entire book story, the same basic ingredients are used. Just a matter of how big of a cake you want to bake.

It's the same recipe for a major motion picture, just enlarge the measurements, or reduce them for smaller story.

It's' my opinion that even one single sentence can have story within it. *"I drew hard on a deep breath, and lept in for the kids."* That single short 13 word sentence has a hero, a challenge, a time crunch, and multiple people to impact and therefore emotional pull.

It paints a basic picture well enough. It's a little 13 word story. Which could also be a story within a bigger story. You get the idea. Stories are not that complicated, but they can be when you want them to be. It's the descriptive language that often brings them to life. Engaging the readers sensory brain regions as we saw earlier. **Giving the elements of the story a sound, a texture, a color, a motion, a smell, a 3 dimensional visual image, a taste and a feel.**

If a story can be made in a single sentence, then one could solidly be made in a paragraph. And if in a paragraph, then in any copy.

The irresistible pull of a story. (It's why TV was invented.)

Ever wonder why TV is almost all story based? Why isn't it just broadcasting a bunch of streaming facts? Why not psychedelic art. Why not numbers and definitions? Why not flashing fireworks all the time? Because **we love stories**. We need stories. We are stories.

Just stating fact is dry copy. Might as well email our list a dictionary. State purposeful *facts* weaved into tantalizing juicy stories. Dripping with hued emotional flavor. Our readers are people, not computers, (Except for Al Gore... Oh I'm just kidding. Maybe:) So facts without stories might miss their target. A readers life is a story, they think, speak and listen best in a story format.

When you were a no taller than your dad's belt, a little pee wee, or tiny chipmunk sized baby girl, what did you love at bed time? "Mommy, Daddy tell me a story." Remember that? We love stories. Love, love love. It starts then. What did you love to do when mommy or daddy was telling you a story? Ask ridiculous questions, right? Like, "Why?"

Questions invite readers to experience the story and play a part in it. That experience, triggers a range of emotions as well. Emotions that have inspired them, since they were too young to read. Compelling story based messages create an **experience,** in a variety of ways. This is where you're previous building blocks in the question Chapters 13,14 and 15 come in.

They provide you the resources to make a *"vegetable soup"* story. The pieces you've learned can all fit together in many ways, depending on your story *experience* objectives.

Our brain loves experiences to the point of risking even death sometimes to get them. Jumping off of mountains, bridges, buildings. One guy strapped a bunch of weather balloons to a lawn chair and flew 1600 feet high. They called him "lawn chair Larry". His bare necessity supplies included beer and a BB gun. They shut down an LA airport because of him. People do crazy things to have an *experience.*

Face mask on? Flippers on? Because we're gong for a swim. Follow me..

High visibility versus Low visibility copy

(Plain sight versus super cool Stealth mode)

Maintain your balance, while sticking your toe in the water here. Then we'll wade on out into the deep bountiful waters of these *writing concepts.* Applying it to Story.

There are situations where I **don't** want to make things too clear. Murky water holds mystery, danger and suspense. Could be a shark out there. Who knows if you can't see it. Right?

Seeing shadow can deliver more fear than seeing the actual being creating the shadow. Right? Hearing a creaking floor might alarm you more than seeing what made it creak. Not knowing, can be a powerful tool for a content writer to use. Do you love watching a movie more, when you know the entire plot in advance, or when you get to see it unfold piece by piece? Aren't anticipation and the unexpected twist's, the most exciting moments? I know my answer.

The same can apply to a single line of words. A sentence can be all revealing, or deliberately withhold information. Neural tuned copy has to consider the purpose of each line. Withholding a detail, is adding drama.

This creates mystery and curiosity. It seeds emotional life. A reading *experience* creates an emotional harvest too. One that the reader enjoys picking the fruits of. I'll reveal the *emotional triggers* in about 50 more lines. If you offer clues leading up to the end of the paragraph, you've given the reader incentive. Their investigation into the copy, is being rewarded with captivating revelations. Justifying further investigation. It's part of story telling. Drawing them into the next paragraph. Step by creaky step.

Let the reader start piecing together a story. Let or help them, solve it. Clue by perplexing clue. Create a mystery feel. Use a *discovery* like process. Then give it a twist.

How to use documentary style, in content marketing.

Consider this. Couldn't the many TV documentaries being broadcast today, just tell you the outcome of results at the very beginning of the show? Of course. But it would suck. Instead they build a mystery first, then solve it. They've got what we want. And they know it. It's why they peel the onion off in layers. Not all at once. Low visibility copy reveals one layer at a time. On purpose. They're not hooking us on the results outright, they've landed us with the *experience* of learning the results. The *process* is the experience. Experience sells. It makes the results more believable too.

In your copy's story, use the onion principle. We're not just making an offer or sending a message, we're producing a moment. A moment of emotional impact for the reader. Even onions can make your cry sometimes. Create an experiential immersion. An experience which culminates in a click. It's the same technique used to build a warm rapport for a pre-frame. Any message is delivered better in stages.

The clues we drop are leading them closer and closer to the ultimate experience, the click link usually. Let your competition just make offers. You make stories, with offers in them.

Great copy to me, creates experience, which can more easily conclude with a more tempting offer. They need to sense that clicking the link, will also bring them emotional rewards. Just like our message did. When great copy is achieved, clicking the link becomes a continuation of the reading experience. A continuation of what they should already be feeling. If the read sucked, then likely the click link will too.

Take-Away: Peel the onion, one layer at a time. Create experience. Draw out emotions. A link or offer, can become the best part of that emotional experience.

How do documentaries build addictive story?

Two words. *Questions* and *answers*. And you can do the same thing in your emails or blog.

When asking readers a question, they will instinctively want to find the answer. They want to assemble the story. It's fun. You love it, I love it, almost everyone does.

It's best done in subtle not overt style writing. Questions and answers can be woven into story form. Just like a documentary. Nearly at the end of a paragraph, ask a question.

The question is the one you are planning to answer in the upcoming paragraph. The previous Chapters (13 through 15) suggested four types to choose from. Your email prospects or blog readers will read each new paragraph just to get the answer from that last question in the previous paragraph.

Like a carrot on a string. You like carrots don't you? I got one for you. It's in the next paragraph...come on, here we go.. Do you know how else bait is used to keep your interest?

Think of your paragraph breaks, like a **commercial breaks**, which are also pre-baited. Just like in a documentary. Before a commercial they always set us up for edge-of-our-seat moment.

Create a perceived climactic moment. Create suspense. Do it near the end of your paragraphs. You may be asking yourself, can this technique be overused? Or, will it work indefinitely?

The fact is, it never stops working. Because we never stop loving questions or stories. We love to piece together our stories. Our copy will read like a mystery novel, which the readers find difficult to resist. Trust will build in their minds, each time you answer one of your own questions. Why does trust build?

Because if the question is about your product or offer, it's like a challenge to it. So by raising a possible doubt, you also conclude with a positive answer. Training the reader that your product or offer always winds up winning the challenge. It also presents you as objective. Not as someone that just toots their own horn. Here's an example:

I really wasn't sure how the optimized ad copy would work on facebook. So I ran a test ad for one week. (That was a Phantom question)

The week did surprise me but but not in a good way. The results actually sucked! Little did I know I had mistakenly put the wrong link address into the ad. Once I fixed it the ads brought the best ROI I ever had.

Questions cannot be ignored. It's like a brain reflex. We don't want to ignore them. We want to answer them, to complete the story we've starting building in our minds. Our curiosity cannot be stopped once triggered. Baiting them like that actually makes them hungry for the answer your about to give them. The answer that makes your product or offer a champion.

Hard hitting copy hits harder, with questions. If not outright, it can create questions in the readers mind. Then answers them. Like the example just given. The *Phantom* question from chapter fourteen is perfect for that.

Without using the power of questions, and mystery, we're just *telling* them stuff. Instead of allowing THEM to participate and to draw their own conclusions. Allowing them to tell it to themselves, proves more powerful than us saying it *to* them.

If they come to their own conclusion, we will have gained trust. At that stage, they believe. And that is our goal.

Take-Away: Interlace stories with any of the four types of questions. Questions are used in documentaries with great success. Bait the ends of paragraphs often.

Twenty Seven

Emotional Triggers - The roller coaster ride of great story.
(The *"Screaming Eagle"* of copy)

The strongest pull on a human, is an emotional pull. Emotion types often number in variety from ten to fifteen. Courage, fear, anger, suspense, envy, shame, kindness, sorrow, anticipation, excitement, wonder, surprise, pity, lust, greed, disgust, amusement, discovery and hope are some of them. As we've seen in previous chapters, emotional content gets fast tracked by our brain.

By itself that's great enough news for writers of copy. Emotions are so important to our survival though, that the brain gives them even more prestige's treatment. They receive top shelf priority in our memories, for easier future access and longer retention. Emotional triggers are the bulls-eye of content writing. If our copy is not aiming for the bulls-eye, then it may never achieve it's maximum potential.

Emotions make good wide open targets, for our copy to tap messages into. Here is where we can take story telling to a different level. Separate it from the "me too" marketing pack. A story carries the message in a framework, that is suited for dual levels of communication. Another classic framework for stories is this: Hero, Villain, the Challenge (threat of failure) and the ultimate Victory. It's a common plot used for thousands of years. In fact George Lucas built a couple of mega-movies using the concept. People relate those plots and characters to their own lives. (more on that in Chapter Twenty Nine). A paragraph in my view can be like a mini story, within a larger story.

Tactical questions can be used to build emotional high and low points. From earlier chapters, you know these types. The *Open* question, the *Leading* question, the *Phantom* question and the *Double Barreled* question. The beginning and mid point of our paragraphs can be used for the *high* points. Positive heightened emotions. The end section is used for the threat of failure - the lows. Suspense moments. Drama where our just proven concept, now faces a challenge. A challenge which could very well defeat the concept. Then, at the beginning of the next paragraph the victory may unfold. Leaving you or your product covered in glory.

The exact opposite arrangement could also work. It's the combination of ups and downs that gives it the drama. Without lows, the highs would not give reason to cheer, or appear as lofty. Can't have a top without a bottom. I was tempted here. To throw in a two piece bikini versus one piece joke, but we're about to discuss heavy food in a sentence or two. I didn't think the two subjects went well together:) Do highs and lows not magnify each other? Emotional involvement is incited by contrasting ideas.

It's like the difference between driving through Kansas or driving through the Rocky Mountains. Which would you rather experience?

Fattened conflict, calls a reader's name. To dine on a delightfully emotional dish. One they're often craving. Emotional food. In the past people have traveled great lengths to get such meals. It means, emotional food satisfies a hunger in our mind, in the same way physical food does for our bodies. We fancy indulgent measures of emotions. It's why we get married, have kids, get pets, watch movies, read books...ahemm (clears throat..:-).

Take-Away: Readers love emotional stories. The emotional ups and downs is like an emotionally scenic drive. Kansas terrain might not have the same affect.

In Allenton Missouri, at Six Flags over Mid-America Amusement Park, they had a roller coaster justly titled *"Screaming Eagle"* . (The screaming that I heard, was no eagle.) People love emotional highs and even emotional fears. If they didn't, amusement parks would be out of business. Our messages, can build their own emotional coaster track. Even if our message is about *"how-to's"* or *"informational copy"*. Copy can have it's own, loop-the-loops, and dead drops. Readers can't help but be moved by suspense, curiosity, victory and a dozen other varieties of emotion . (And come back paying for more.) We're all crazy like that.

For example, a question that suggests a real problem or obstacle which our product might not be able to handle. The question is placed after a positive stretch of copy. The reader experiences a mini emotional roller coaster. With highs strategically placed. Then the lows that we are triggering - just when they thought it's safe to go back into the water. That type of product set up probably won't cause a major back flip out of their chair, but it could help to keep them reading and remember what they've read. Remember from previous chapters, emotions are linked to memories. Feeling your copy means they will remember it. Which is where every author, marketer or message writer dreams of living. In their readers memory.

It might help to know how our brain processes and measures emotions. There are three main filters it uses. Positive versus negative is one. The intensity of the emotion is another. And whether the emotions involves another person or not. That's the third.

These were recent findings at Carnegie Mellon University which showed how the brain organizes emotions (Rea, 2013). Intense positive emotion involving another person, would seem to be a beneficial trigger for cognitive activity. That's a good thing, it means they're engaged in our copy. The *happiness* feeling, gave the easiest detectable emotional neural signature.

Take-Away: Intentionally bring readers up with positive, happy copy, then shift it to another direction. In doing this, each paragraph delivers an emotional dynamic. Like a mini-story. After several paragraphs, momentum of "challenge and victory" pattern is established. Our reader will have witnessed, and felt multiple challenges and victories (to us or our product). Making our product or offer seem more invincible. More compelling.

Twenty Eight

The E word. (And the L word.)

Why is emotional and sensory activity so important to a message? One word. **EXPERIENCE**. They create a sense of emotional <u>experience</u> in our copy. Well, what's so big about experience? Experience equals reality. It's how we distinguish fake-ality from reality. Our senses.

Reality is believable. So if your message takes on realities characteristics, it becomes believable. That's what's so big about *experience*.

Experience is what we're really selling, and what motivates our reader to click, opt in, or buy. We don't pay $5.00 for a cup of coffee at Starbucks. We pay $5.00 for the Starbucks coffee experience.

It makes you feel good about you. It's what we're all after deep down. To feel good about ourselves. If you really want to know the truth, it's so that we feel <u>loved</u>. That innate drive of wanting to feel loved, is at the center of everything we do. This was the message that created a giant nine digit tidal wave of money for one great visionary. Empowering millions people to live happy and successful lives too.

The Giant inside you. That what Tony Robbins brings out.

You've no doubt heard of a little fella' named Tony Robbins? Big heart, big dreams. Underlying his corporations $500,000,000 worth, and his life's passion, is that simple little theory. **We do what we do, because we want to feel <u>loved</u>.** Often we don't see that, but if we look closer, it's really there. Tony's got some great books out that can detail it very well.

Tony, broke with psychology's convention when his studies revealed to him some short cuts to reach life's greatest goals. The result -- he did what few others have ever been able to do, in terms of helping people achieve. Presidents, billion dollar execs', sports heroes, he's helped them all. He broke free from the pack. Taught it his way.

Tony bypassed college. Yet his passion for true understanding (as opposed to conventional teachings) led him to read 700 books. I'd call it the "college of Barnes and Noble."

Stepping out, he took his skill to a another level. Yep, this psycologosifhy stuff really works. By the way, he's got a great *"story"* that helped build his two comma empire. And he tells it often. About his meager beginnings and living out of his car. Our love of stories, helped build Tony's dream. It helped because we bought into his great story, to the tune of $500,000,000. That's a lot of love, both ways.

So then, what's the heart all this fancy brain research?

Facts bore us. Because they only arouse one section of our brain. Lefty loves facts, but just facts are boring righty. Unless of coarse, the facts are woven into emotional and sensory rich story form! If facts become part of an experience, then facts are like lasers that burn through anything. When we build that type of copy, multiple neural resources are engaged.

If we want to engage the full brain of our readers, and not bore them to misery- -use *story* based facts. Not just lone facts. Use questions and answers. Find creative ways to insert the facts, so they are emotionally tied to the story. Tied to the questions. Use a documentary feel to slam dunk your copy.

Take-Away: Better not to just write lone facts. Mix in story elements. We create *Experience* for the reader, in our story. Experienced facts become reality. Use multisensory triggers to fill bring facts to life. Experience is what were really selling. Facts are used to help us anchor our story.

I had to fire the dude! *(But my customers loved him..)*

In my first business, back in the 80's I learned a lesson which has never escaped me. And changed my marketing forever. One of my employees, who's name we'll call Gerg. I've cleverly disguised his name by rearranging the letters in it. To protect his true identity.... :)

Gave him a company car. Gave him free reign, out on his own. But he wouldn't come to work on time if at all. It was a service business, and this guy also couldn't fix much right. To me, it was shaping up to be total mishap waiting to happen. The strangest thing though. My customers would always ask for Greg, ooops, I mean Gerg.

They loved him. He was nice. I liked him too. Because they loved him, they also referred their friends to use my business. As much as I hated to admit it, Gerg was a customer magnet. He was just so nice, and friendly. Loved to talk all the way through the job. (when he was supposed to be working) It's why he couldn't fix anything. Never focused on the problem which they called him to fix.

Oddly, they didn't seem to care. Whether it got fixed or not, they were still happy. As long as it was Gerg that showed up. He couldn't fix things because he was too focused on being friends with the customer. That's what they loved. He made them feel good, about them selves. (Remember Tony's love principle?) By giving them his attention, and just being like-able. By making them feel good, they didn't seem to care that his mechanical skills sucked. They liked him, which created trust.

It proves the effect that changing a persons state of mind can have, on how they perceive you, or your service, or your product, **or your copy,** (Even your credentials.). People interpret our messages partly based on how they feel, and especially how they *feel about us.*

Eventually I had to let him go, because he wouldn't show up to work. I couldn't let appointments not be kept. Wasn't fair to my customers. It's a marketing lesson I never forgot though. How emotions and the subconscious mind, can override good sense.

N fact the brain sends information faster to our emotional trigger areas, than to our rational thought regions. It's a powerful copy writing lesson. People want to feel loved. It's a great **experience,** to feel loved. Gerg made them feel that, and they responded to it.

And I responded, by firing Gerg ... (It's not funny I know, but it's late, I'm tired and getting slap happy! The story about what happened is a little funny though, in my review mirror at least....Quit looking at me like that! I'm not proud of it you know! Let's just move on;).

Take away: Making our reader happy and feel good, like a friend, can outweigh the actual offer. It can even overcome less than perfect products and services. People want to feel good, more than anything.

Twenty Nine

Our love of stories, built Apple. Apple? Yep, Apple.

Ultra successful businesses are often built, by the deliberate insertion of stories. Steve Jobs story embodies our perception of Apple products. *"Think different"* is a two word brand story. It's meaning was directly linked to Steve Jobs personal story. We remember Steve's story when we think of Apple products. We feel a little bit like Steve, when we use them. It's weird but true. In a way he was a very envied person. Using his products brings a little piece of that into our own life.

Something strange happens when we read or watch a story. A subconscious internal transformation occurs. At least that's what a number of scientist theorized.

Atlanta Georgia 2013. Emory University discovered a phenomenon which occurred in readers of a novel. By using brain image mapping over a period of 19 consecutive days, they found our <u>identities</u> may be altered by what we read.

Neuro-scientist Gregory Berns, said *"..neural changes we found associated with physical sensation and movement systems, suggest that reading a novel can transport you [mentally]into the body of the protagonist* [main character]". This is why I suggested that we feel a little bit like the late Steve Jobs, when we use Apple products.

Certain brain regions returned to base line activity, shortly after the reading stopped. Other brain regions, showed longer term connectivity changes. They *"persisted for several days after the reading"*. Researchers termed this finding **"embodied semantics"**. What's that mean? To me, it meas we identify with the character we read about. The report was published in *"Brain Connectivity"*. So, here we have more evidence that confirms what most of us already felt.

As a kid, me and my friends used to watch football scenes in slow motion. Snow falling in the game, and them champions on TV were muddied up, sailing through the air over the top of surprised opponents. First thing we did was go out side in the yard and pretend we were them. Give ourselves the same names, as the players we just watched on TV. At least I did. In our minds, we were now the hero's we just watched on TV. Even tried to fall in slow motion, like we saw them do on TV.

After watching Rocky, as an adult, I remember getting a speed bag. In my mind, when I was tr*ying* to build up a fast rhythm, I'd think of Rocky. Somehow merging him and me in my mind as if I had the same drive he had. As if we were in some small way the same. So, I can relate to the study at Emory. It rings true to my own experiences. Making it a strong belief in me.

In short, **we become the character we read about.** To a degree of course. Most amazingly, we even stay the character we read about, at least for a little while. Even for days, according to the study.

Our readers, internally identify with our story. Purchasers of Apple products, identity with Steve Jobs. N fact our reason for purchasing Apple products, may be linked to a subconscious belief. A belief that a little bit of the coolness of the product (and Steve) may spill over onto us. We feel a little bit cooler with an iPhone or iPad. Why do you think people camp out to get the new Apple products on the very first day? We want so badly to be associated with coolness. To be associated with what people love. I have a question for you. An *open* one.

It's just something to think about. If readers are NOT given a story or character in our copy to identify with, then what in our copy would they identify with? Would it mean that we lose the power of personal connection with them? Again, like fishing without a hook. Sort of like fishing without a personal hook for them to connect to? If the need to identify with us, is actually important. Then wouldn't that make a story or character in our copy, equally important? Not suggesting I know the answer, but it seems worth considering.

Some copywriters have collected dozens of millions of dollars, by building themselves into a marketable character in their content. Character development should be part of every email campaign. Each email should be part of a string, and each linking the ongoing story to each other. And the center of that campaign should be the main character of the ongoing story, you. If not you, then some form of character that the reader wants to relate to.

Back to the speed bag.

Most of us have heard the story of Sylvester Stallone and how it played a role in the making of *Rocky*. You know the one. Where he had to sell his dog to buy food. And he refused to sell the script unless he got to play the leading roll. Even though he needed the money. Then he bought the dog back when he got the roll and sold the script. Only he had to pay thousands more to get the dog back from the same guy. Supposedly the same dog that wound up playing in the movie. Butkis.

Only problem is, **the story was fake**. It was fabricated to drive sales. A marketing stunt, or so I heard. They did it because they knew a story would drive sales. It did. Even the movie itself is based on a great story. An unknown faces impossible challenges, stuns the world, and becomes champion of it. I loved it. Stories sell. The reason they sell, is because we identify with them. Connecting our own challenges and obstacles to theirs. And if they could make it, then so can we.

Virgin is another story built business. Richard Branson's long hair and on-the-edge life style, is synonymous with their branding. Also with their business philosophies. Just like Apple and Jobs. **Our love of stories, built Apple, Virgin, Tony Robbins empire and Sylvester Stallone's career,** if you really think about it.

"The best brands are built on great stories". Ian Rowden, chief marketing officer, *Virgin Group*.

Take-Away: Use story within the copy. It could be the most important part. Great brands use stories. We can give our readers a story they will want to identify with. Hero, nemesis, challenge and victory.

Thirty

Recon homework of your own. (The fun kind:)

I've got some fun assignments for you. (Not really assignments. More like experiments and great learning tricks that have helped me.)

If you choose to take these *missions,* and wind up getting caught, I will disavow all knowledge of giving them to you. That last sentence and this one, will self destruct once you close this book.

Some home work for later-- maybe <u>write this part down.</u> (It may help you follow through. If you're like me, writing things down, gives them the strongest chance of getting done.).

Watch at least 1 hour of the history channel (*The "Mysteries at the Museum" is one I learn from*). Focus on how they use questions and answers to create suspense and engagement. Notice how they withhold information until they want you to have it. Seeing it and feeling it working on you, will lock the technique into your brain. It was a real eye-opener for me.

Listen to two songs of your choice, focusing on how many words are in each lyrical phrase. Focus also on the music in the background . How it creates mood, for the lyrics. One I enjoy is Secret Garden by Springsteen. One of my fav's.

Read at least one chapter of "The Finisher". David Baldacci is a master at writing pictures. Read at least one chapter in one of Veronica Roth's books, *Divergent* or *Insurgent.*

Don't forget to bring your favorite pen and notebook. It's a smorgasbord of writing knowledge that is piled high and deep. Scoop yourself off some good pointers, from two proven masters of words. They sell a lot of books, so you know that people love the way they write. You might be able to cop a free preview on Amazon or at Barnes and Noble.

This is one is my favorite: **Give a warm sincere smile, to a complete stranger**, while looking directly in their eyes. For instance in a checkout lane, as your leaving a store and saying "thank you". Watch the reaction you get back and how you changed that persons demeanor and state instantly. It works the same way in copy. It's that right brain language at work. Doing it in person, with a real smile will solidify your belief that the face and feel of your copy is incredibly important to the readers right brain hemisphere. **Do that to 3 different people**. It revealed to me what a powerful way of communicating to the right brain is.

***

That's it. Did I keep my promise in showing you some cool stuff? hope so, and am so glad you took your valuable time to read my book.

If I did keep my promise, please go ahead and share what you enjoyed, with someone else. Spread the love.

Enjoyed sharing this stuff with you. Hey, stop by the site JohnKrone.com and sign up to get any new content opportunities, as I put them out. (If you haven't signed up already). More stuff in the works too. I'll hit you back on it when ever I'm feeling it's right.

Hey, your voice is important, I'd love to hear what you thought of this book. Others may too.

Find my newest original content at JohnKrone.com

My *End Notes*:

My style: I like to write my basic sentence while it's in my head, using basic language. Then go back and improve it, using the principles in this book afterwards. May take a few times. I find that easier and more fun, than trying to get it perfect, on the first run. Printing out the Cheat Sheet in the next chapter, and keeping it on your desk, can be an easy way to help trigger your own memory. Calling on that amazing writing knowledge now residing in your mental vault. Spread the love **JohnKrone.com**

The End (And the beginning of your improved skills.)

***

Thirty One

Optimizer Cheat Sheet - Power Tweaks

(The Take-Aways.)

This Optimizer Cheat Sheet is like a ***Textual Blue-Print.*** It's a quick-reference guide, for emails, web pages, books, blog posts and ads. It can be implemented like an action plan. By applying all of the techniques it will neural tune your copy. Use it like a Check-List

Optimizer Cheat Sheet.

Take-Away: Page color, font Style, imagery and shapes are the 1st thing the reader sees. They are your FIRST headline. They pre-frame the textual headline. Write copy for *both conscious and unconscious* levels of perception. Do this by using all of the techniques. Target both left and right brain awareness. More brain regions activated, means a more mentally engaged reader. Chapter 2

Take Away: The readers *right brain radar* will bust mixed or confused messages. Compelling copy should speak the same message on both perception levels. Presentation colors, fitting style, feel, imagery, shapes etc. are monitored by RBR (Right Brain Radar). Use them as a pre-frame for your written content Presentation must pre-frame and compliment the written message. If not you have the Stroop effect. Chapter 4.

Take-Away: Create Multi-sensory reading experience. *Different words* cause our brain to activate different regions, depending on the words. The words we choose to write in copy, are sent to different places in the readers brain. Determined by the exact word chosen. This knowledge, gives us incredible power. Power to *deliberately target specific brain regions.* Chapter 7.

Scent -Taste - Color

Take Away- Include scent words. *Scent.* The word "cookie", activates the same part of the brain as a real cookie. *Scent* related copy does two things. Creates a present sensory experience, and recalls emotional memories connected to those scents. It adds emotional, historical and sensory dimension to our copy. Enriching reader experience. Making our copy more believable. Chapter 7.

Take-Away: Using scent related words, activates emotions. Emotions are processed faster than rational thought and stored longer, increasing retention of our copy. Chapter 7.

Take Away: Include color words, whenever it applies. *Color words* (red, blue, yellow etc.) activate the same multiple parts of the brain as seeing the color itself. Use them to create a colored picture in the readers "Mind's Eye". Chapter 7.

Take-Away: Match Color words to Scent words. *Activate more* reader brain regions, to engage the reader. Do it by inserting *sensory rich words*. Compliment scent related copy with their associated color words, to intensify the impact of both. *Taste* suited color words, also intensify *taste* related messages. Targeting multiple senses, creates multidimensional copy. Chapter 7.

Take-Away: Don't mis-match Color and Scent words. *Wrong color matching*, (mismatched color to scent or taste) detracts from the neural intensity of both.. Chapter 7.

Focus -Fresh -Positive - Emotional Verbs.

Take-Away: Fade the outside world, by controlling their focus with engaging sensory rich content. *Control their focus* by creating a compelling textual environment. One that keeps the readers senses fully captivated. Triggering multiple sensory targets, fades the outside world. Keeps their focus on our message. Influencing their focus, improves how our primary message touches them. The *"textual world"* we create within their mind, sets the believability stage, for our primary message. The same message in the distracting environment, could strike their eyes as less believable. Chapter 9.

Take-Away: No Stale overused language. *"Just say No"* - to *stale* words or phrases. Keep it *fresh* and *unexpected.* Keep em' guessing. Choose words that they don't see coming. Rephrase and refresh. Overplayed language bores the readers brains. (Especially righty). Chapter 10.

Take-away: Be Positive, not negative. To get deeper brain connection, *keep it positive*. Negative words turn the lights off, in our readers brain. To bypass the brains protective shielding and promote conversion, promote the positive only. Chapter 11.

Take-Away: Use Emotional verbs for a physical response. Emotional verbs give one of the strongest pushes. They lead to physical action. Conversion can be increased by introducing verbs into our call to action. Add an emotional sensory dimension to your message and trigger physical muscle reactions. Letting the reader feel the action, and take action. Chapter 12.

Questions

Take-Away: Use Open question as end of paragraph. Mentally chain the reader to your copy by ending the paragraph with an *Open question*. Open questions leave a wide opening for a variety of answers. (Rather than a Yes or No answer, which limits their participation). Chapter 13.

Take-Away: Use *Loaded Leading* questions to prompt the reader to <u>recall</u> what they already believe, from past experiences. An armor piercing *recall* persuasion tool. Chapter 14.

Take-Away: Use a *Phantom* question to get the reader to ask you a question. It's an answer they will be eager to pursue. Do this, by introducing curiosity. Make an inconclusive statement, and leave them hanging. Just until the next paragraph or two. Example: *"The results were something I never expected".* Chapter 13.

Take Away: Use *Compound* questions to introduce a challenge, or possibility of doubt for your product or message. It creates drama. It will slip in and slice the sales pressure cord cleanly. That cord could have pulled the reader away from you. Best of all your upcoming answer will make the product or message look victorious. It occurs when you answer the question positively in the next paragraph or two. Chapter 15.

Periods - Micro Sentences - Longer Sentences.

Take-Away: Use *Short sentences* at the beginning of paragraphs, Always weigh the cost of long sentences. Readers prefer less not more. Split your sentence in two, or shorten it when ever possible. Makes easier absorption. More believable. Use the *period*, liberally. Chapter 16.

Take-Away: Use a *Micro sentence* to put a punch in your main finishing points. It delivers powerful concluding impact. Use to start a new paragraph. It also makes an inviting welcome mat. Chapter 17.

Take Away: Use *Longer sentences* to compose pictures and scenes. Spin visual and emotional moments. Create dimensional aspects using descriptive language. Depth, height, feel, color, scent, sound, movement, touch. Chapter 13.

Trust - Forced Agreement - Authority - Associations

Take-Away: Try to establish trust early on in the message. Everything else we have to say or offer, hinges on trust. Trust pre-framing gives advantage to the rest of our message. Chapter 20

Take -Away: For *Trust*. Force the reader to agree with you early on, by stating some facts. Chapter 21.

Take -Away: For *Trust,* establish authority. Introduce polite commands. Be cool about it though. Chapter 21.

Take-Away: For *Trust,* use *Associations*. Three step association method is: *Logical* connection to you, create a textual *3D image* description of the association, *recall* it within 30 seconds of read time. Hammer it home with repetition. Use story form to deliver the message. Meaning, imagery, sound and a hammer. <u>Chapter 22</u>.

Take-Away: Pre-frame your content --Use *"Thank You"* and *"I'm sorry"*, sincerely. Other kindness works too. They work well in the first line or two of your copy. It earns you respect and trust. Humble yourself and they will too. <u>Chapter 22</u>.

Emotions - Happy - Positive - Mood - Relaxed Environment

Take Away: Use e*motional* content to create a relaxed mood in the person reading. A readers relaxed state of mind, activates more brain regions (i.e more engaged reader). Emotional content, gets our message processed faster (because it's given a higher priority) and it's remembered longer. Up to 1 year, and kept in storage up to a lifetime. <u>Chapter 23</u>.

Take-Away: Stimulating the readers *happy emotion.* This influences *where* their brain sends the message. It determines how well they receive it, altering perception of our copy, offer, and call to action. They interpret messages, based on the particular *emotional* slant we give it. <u>Chapter 24</u>.

Take-Away: Set up the e*nvironment* and state of our reader, to fit the message. It will unite right and left brain senses. (fun, excited or curious states are also pleasurable states). A pleasurable relaxed state increases brain activity while reading. Create a sensory rich environment with colors and general feel of our copy. One that suites the primary message or offer. <u>Chapter 25</u>.

Story - Peel the Onion - Interlace 4 types of Questions -Ups and Downs - Facts with Story

Take-Away: Peel the onion, one layer at a time. Create experience. Draw out emotions. A link or offer, can become part of that emotional experience. <u>Chapter 26</u>.

Take-Away: Use documentary style stories. Interlace stories with any of the four types of questions. Questions are used in documentaries with great success. <u>Chapter 26</u>.

Take-Away: Use emotional stories. Readers love emotional stories. The emotional ups and downs is like an emotionally scenic drive. Kansas terrain might not have the same affect. <u>Chapter 27</u>.

Take-Away: Intentionally bring readers up with positive, happy copy, then shift

it to another direction. In doing this, each paragraph delivers an emotional dynamic. Drama. Like a mini-story. After several paragraphs, momentum of "challenge and victory" pattern is established. Our reader will have witnessed, and felt multiple challenges and victories (to us or our product). Making our product or offer seem more invincible. More compelling. <u>Chapter 27</u>.

Experience - Love -Friendly

Take-Away: Better not to just write lone facts. Mix in story elements. We create *Experience* for the reader, in our story. Experienced facts become reality. Use multisensory triggers to fill bring facts to life. Experience is what were really selling. Facts are used to help us anchor our story. <u>Chapter 28</u>.

Take away: Making our reader happy and feel good, like a friend, can outweigh the actual offer. It can even overcome less than perfect products and services. People want to feel good, more than anything. <u>Chapter 28</u>.

Take-Away: Use story and character development within the copy. It could be the most important part. Great brands use stories. We can give our readers a story they will want to identify with. (Hero, nemesis, challenge, countdown and victory) <u>Chapter 29</u>.

I'll expect to be hearing good reports on your optimized, neural tuned high performance copy. Tweak your copy and rock some sales!

JohnKrone.com

Bibliography and References

aps."Smile as you read this:Language that puts you in touch with your bodily feellings"Association for Psychological science.(visit 3.10.2015) <http://www.psychologicalscience.org/index.php/news/releases/smile-as-you-read-this-language-that-puts-you-in-touch-with-your-bodily-feelings.html>(n.d.)

Ascend2,"Few eople Trust Social Media Marketing..."(visit 2014)<http://ascend2.com/home/programs/>(main site)

Baldacci, David."The finisher". Columbus Rose ltd. Scholastic Inc.2014. (3.22.2015)<www.amazon.com/Finisher-Vega-Jane-Book/dp/054565226X/ref=sr_1_1?ie=UTF8&qid=1427034532&sr=8-1&keywords=david+baldacci+finisher>

Bohannon, John Huffington Post Huff Post Science "Facial expressions:Smiles, frowns not universal after all, study suggests" (2014)<http://www.huffingtonpost.com/2012/04/18/facial-expression-culture-_n_1434175.html>(2012, April 18)

Clark, Roy Poynter "Suspense...and the short sentence" 2014<http://www.poynter.org/how-tos/newsgathering-storytelling/writing-tools/79789/suspense-and-the-short-sentence/>(2006, Dec 14)

Clark, Roy The New York Times "The short sentence as Gospel Truth" (2014<http://opinionator.blogs.nytimes.com/2013/09/07/the-short-sentence-as-gospel-truth/?_php=true&_type=blogs&_r=0>(2013, Sept 7)

Clark,Dick.The 2008 Time 100, Jill Bolte TaylorTime. online mageine. Science and Thinkers magazine<http://content.time.com/time/specials/2007/article/0,28804,1733748_1733754_1735155,00.html>(2008, May 12)

Dolcos, Florin Lordan, Alexandru D, Dolcos, Sanda Journal of Cognitive Psychology Best Paper Award 2011. "Neural correlates of emotion -- cognition interactions..."(2014)<http://dolcoslab.beckman.illinois.edu/files/Dolcos-Iordan-Dolcos_2011_JCP_Emo-Cog_Review.pdf>(2011)

Green, KJ.[video]"Navy Seals Mental Training" clip from "The Brain" History Channel. (4/012014)<https://www.youtube.com/watch?v=Ju4FojRkEKU>(2012 Feb 12)

Hopkins, Claude C."Scientific Advertising"Palmera Publishing.1923

Leaf, Caroline Dr."Who switched off my brain?"Inprov, ltd. 2009.Amazon link<http://www.amazon.com/Who-Switched-Off-Brain-Revised/dp/0981956726/ref=sr_1_1?ie=UTF8&qid=1427036932&sr=8-1&keywords=who+shut+off+my+brain>

John Krone - Word-Power 33 Ways to write more convincing emails, blogs and books

Huntsberget, Brent."Nike 'Just Do It' slogan celebrates 20 years.Oregon Business News.(retrieved 2/2/2015)<http://www.oregonlive.com/business/oregonian/index.ssf?/base/business/1216353305226620.xml>(2008, July 18)

LiveScience staff"Brains of bilingual readers repress negative words" NBCNEWS.The Body Odd. (visited 3/22/2015)<http://bodyodd.nbcnews.com/_news/2012/05/08/11605196-brains-of-bilingual-readers-repress-negative-words?lite>(2012,May 8)

Taylor, Jill."Jill Bolt Taylor Stroke of insight" [video]<https://www.youtube.com/watch?v=UyyjU8fzEYU>(Jan.1.2013)(2008,March 13)

Taylor, Jill Bolte. Jill Bolte Taylor Book on Amazon. "My Stroke of Insight:A brain scientist's personal journey." Penguin Group 2009.<http://www.amazon.com/My-Stroke-Insight-Scientists-Personal/dp/0452295548/ref=sr_1_1?s=books&ie=UTF8&qid=1426995115&sr=1-1&keywords=jill+bolte+taylor>

Taylor, Jill Bolte. website<http://mystrokeofinsight.com/>

Paul, Annie Murphy."Your Brain on Fiction".The New York Times Sunday Review<http://www.nytimes.com/2012/03/18/opinion/sunday/the-neuroscience-of-your-brain-on-fiction.html?_r=0>(Feb 1 2013) 2012, March 17

"Stroop effect",n.d.(3/22/2015)<http://en.wikipedia.org/wiki/Stroop_effect>

Stefan, Frank L."The ERP response to the amount of information conveyed by words in sentences."Bran and Language.(viewed 3/22/2015) <http://www.sciencedirect.com/science/article/pii/S0093934X14001515>(2015, Jan)

Rea, Shilo "Carnegie Mellon Researchers Identify Emotions based on brain activity.".Carnegie Mellon News.(visited 3/12/2015)<http://www.cmu.edu/news/stories/archives/2013/june/june19_identifyingemotions.html>(2013, June 19)

White, T.H."The Sword In The Stone".1938.(visited 3/02/215)<http://en.wikipedia.org/wiki/The_Sword_in_the_Stonehttp://en.wikipedia.org/wiki/The_Sword_in_the_Stone>

Atsumi Toshiko, Tonosaki Keiichi "Smelling lavender and rosemary increases free radical scavenging activity and decreases cortisol level in saliva" (2014)

John Krone - Word-Power 33 Ways to write more convincing emails, blogs and books

<http://www.researchgate.net/publication/6512802_Smelling_lavender_and_rosemary_increases_free_radical_scavenging_activity_and_decreases_cortisol_level_in_saliva>(2007)

Kadohisa, Mikiko "Effects of odor on emotion, with implications" 2015
<http://www.ncbi.nlm.nih.gov/pmc/articles/PMC3794443/>(2013, Oct 10)

Cromie, William J "Harvard University Gazette "Brain's color processor is located"(2014)<http://www.news.harvard.edu/gazette/1998/08.06/BrainsColorProc.html>(1998, August 6)

Österbauer Robert A, Paul M. Matthews , Mark Jenkinson , Christian F. Beckmann , Peter C. Hansen , Gemma A. Calvert Journal of Neurophysiology "Color of Scents: Chromatic Stimuli Modulate Odor Responses in the Human Brain "(2014)<http://jn.physiology.org/content/93/6/3434>(2005, June 1)

emotiv 2014<http://www.emotiv.com/>

Huntsberget, Brent."Nike 'Just Do It' slogan celebrates 20 years.Oregon Business News.(retrieved 2/2/2015)<http://www.oregonlive.com/business/oregonian/index.ssf?/base/business/1216353305226620.xml>(2008, July 18)
2014<http://abcnews.go.com/blogs/health/2012/05/10/font-size-matters-says-study/>

Robbins, Anthony "Change your focus-- rethink your to-do list" (2015)<http://training.tonyrobbins.com/change-your-focus-rethink-your-to-do-list/>

Orwelle, George The literature network. "Shooting and elephant" (2015)<http://www.online-literature.com/orwell/887/

Eastman Quinn Emory news center "Say it with Feeling" (2014)<http://news.emory.edu/stories/2012/02/metaphor_brain_imaging/campus.html> (2012, Feb 8)

Cherry, Steven, Sathian, Krish interview. "IEEE Spectrum "This is your brain on metaphor"(2014)<http://spectrum.ieee.org/podcast/biomedical/imaging/this-is-your-brain-on-metaphor>(2012, Apr 6)

Wansink, Brian, James Painter, and Koert van Ittersum (2001), "Descriptive Menu Labels' Effect on Sales," (2014)<http://foodpsychology.cornell.edu/pdf/pre-prints/descriptivemenulabels-2001.pdf>(2001, December)

Wlotko, Edward W, Federmeier, Kara D "NCBI Finding the right word: Hemispheric Asymmetries in the use of sentence context information".

John Krone - Word-Power 33 Ways to write more convincing emails, blogs and books

(2014)<http://www.ncbi.nlm.nih.gov/pmc/articles/PMC2066191/>(2007, Jun 8)

Font Size(2014)<http://abcnews.go.com/blogs/health/2012/05/10/font-size-matters-says-study/>

Compwell, Complete Wellbeing "How the brain reacts to negative language!"
(2014)<http://completewellbeing.com/wellbeing-news/how-the-brain-reacts-to-negative-language/>2012, May 15)

Live Science staff , NBC News, The body odd, "Brains of bilingual readers repress negative words"
(2014)<http://bodyodd.nbcnews.com/_news/2012/05/08/11605196-brains-of-bilingual-readers-repress-negative-words?lite>(2012, May 8)

Goldman, Corrie, Stanford News "This is your brain on Jane Austen, and Stanford researchers taking notes" (2014)<http://news.stanford.edu/news/2012/september/austen-reading-fmri-090712.html>(2012, Sept 7)

www.ingramcontent.com/pod-product-compliance
Lightning Source LLC
Chambersburg PA
CBHW070815180526
45168CB00002B/627